Inspirational Thoughts

Doris Cowen

WESTBOW
PRESS
A DIVISION OF THOMAS NELSON

WestBow Press books may be ordered through booksellers or by contacting:

WestBow Press
A Division of Thomas Nelson
1663 Liberty Drive
Bloomington, IN 47403
www.westbowpress.com
1-(866) 928-1240

ISBN: 978-1-4497-7287-1 (sc)

Library of Congress Control Number: 2012920879

Printed in the United States of America

WestBow Press rev. date: 11/06/2012

Inspirational Thoughts

By Doris Cowen

To my readers,

God has his own timetable with everyone's life. Over a lifetime of wanting to be an author of Christian writing, this book finally came into being. About thirty years ago, I did "Dial-a-Devotion" that I recorded each week and this helped me grow spiritually. During the next 10 years I cared for my Mother who was an invalid by that time. God taught me many things. After her death in 1999, I started writing "Inspirational Thoughts" for the Democrat-Argus, our weekly newspaper. This has been many years of learning and enjoying my work. All my life, I have felt that God had special work for me to do. Many times, writing these stories in the wee hours of the morning, I have felt God's Presence, guidance and inspiration. Without Him there would have been no stories. My prayer is that these stories will be a blessing to everyone who reads them.

– *Doris Cowen*

I want to give a special thanks to my new friend, Susie Robison, who helped me to get this book ready to be published. Without her knowledge of computers and her willingness to help others, this book might still be waiting to be heard.

Table of Contents

Table of Contents

"God's Love Is Everywhere"

God's love has no boundaries such as we use – north, south, east, or west. It cannot be measured by depth – that is distance measured downward, inward or backward. Height does not apply here – God's love has no marked measure of altitude. In fact, everything holds together because His love formed this world and everything in it for us because we are His children.

We do not hold the key to our existence here. Only the love of God keeps us going from day to day. We walk the road of life because He holds our hand – we laugh, think and talk because He keeps our inner mechanism working. Were He to let go of us, we would be unable to function as the persons we are.

It is hard for me to grasp that God loves us as much as the Bible says. Psalm 139 vs. 17, 18, (KJV) reads -

> "How precious also are thy thoughts unto me, O God!
> How great is the sum of them!
> If I should count them, they are more in number than the sand:
> When I awake, I am still with thee."

In our humanity, we believe that when someone thinks of us a lot and wants to make us happy, we feel that we are greatly loved. Isn't this what makes our world hold together? It is so nice to start the day with someone that we love. We go off to work, whatever kind we do, and we strive to succeed. We know that the "top of the ladder" brings its own rewards. But, many of us do not become well known, or rich, or important in the world's eyes. We still labor to bring substance to our world and when love is the guiding factor, we have it all!

God uses the word "precious" several times in His messages to us. This word's meaning is very descriptive. It says that something or someone is of great value to us. Most of us have used this word at times in our own lives when we wanted to say just how much something or someone meant to us. God did this too in Isaiah 43 v 4b (NLT) –
"—- you are precious to me. You are honored, and I love you."

It's a startling thing how God puts His love within us and uses us to touch others. No matter how much we shake hands greeting others; regardless of how many times we touch someone to show love to them; and not counting how many times our hearts fill up with love and concern for others; the supply never runs out. The more love we give away, the more God's love gushes up within us and spills out. It is like we are connected to God's spigot and the supply is endless. But, the paradox of it is that with every iota of love that passes through us, we, ourselves grow hungrier and hungrier to receive as well as to give love. We were made this way, and are meant to live our lives dominated by this emotion. We are short-changing ourselves when love does not open our door in the morning and close our door in the evening. We are losing sight of our birthright when we do not sense God's Presence with us in the night-time as well as in the day-time.

We can't have God without having love and we can't have love without having God!

"I, Myself and Me"

We all have a person living within us that we need to get to know. Who says that only the selfish person attends to one's inner being? Too much attention to individual priorities can be a damaging thing to our personalities but how can we come to love ourselves if we do not know ourselves? To take the inward look can make us know that we are indeed less than perfect and it can also help us realize how much we need God's forgiveness.

We are told repeatedly to love our neighbor as ourselves. His concerns are to be just as important to us as our own. It seems to me that God means for us to put our shoulder to the wheel in his behalf but how we align ourselves to another person should be done under the supervision of the Lord. Only God knows the inner-workings of another heart and only He can direct us as we try to love our neighbor.

Loving ourselves, our neighbors, and even God are lifetime commitments. We are still in this world today because it pleases God to allow it. I have just discovered a new phrase in Ecclesiastes 3:11 – "God has

4

made everything beautiful for its own time. *He has planted eternity in the human heart.*" This is the part of us we need to cultivate – because eternity has been planted here.

Finding time and ways to know ourselves is a constant challenge. I have been so impressed by an advertisement on television that is linked to portraying the Chevrolet Tahoe Truck, the go anywhere, do anything vehicle. This poem was written by Patrick O'Leary for General Motors. After e-mailing several people my request to use this poem was ok'd by Mr. Matthew Banchek, General Motors Officer.

"Nobody Knows It But Me"

"There's a place that I travel
When I want to roam
And nobody knows it but me.

The roads don't go there
And the signs stay home
And nobody knows it but me.

It's far, far away
And way, way afar
It's over the moon and the sea,

And wherever you're going
That's wherever you are
And nobody knows it but me."

Our quiet time with God can help us know "I, Myself and Me!"

"School Days"

"School days, school days,
Dear old golden rule days,
Readin' and 'ritin' and 'rithmetic
Taught to the tune of a hick-ry stick
You were my queen in calico,

5

I was your bashful barefoot beau
And you wrote on my slate, "I love you Joe",
When we were a couple of kids."

This song was written almost 100 years ago – in 1907 to be exact. The music was done by Gus Edwards and the words were written by Will D. Cobb. This was a different time; a different place and a different state of mind.

And yet, down deep, children today bear much similarity to children of 100 years ago. Times were certainly different then – many things we have today were not even imagined in those days. Just think – no television; no air conditioning, no automatic dishwashers, no pizza, no Sealy mattresses, no Toyota cars. In fact, Henry Ford was just beginning to put his ideas into the reality of the automobile.

But, children then had the same inner make-up. Most of them wanted to excel in their studies; they wanted to fit in with their peers, and they wanted to have fun. Perhaps there is more emphasis put on "having fun" today than it was then. But, I believe they had a desire to laugh and to seek freedom in light-heartedness. Everything was just so precise then when compared with the standards of today.

Some of my school friends became life-long friends and our lives were woven together. One person in particular is Betty Ray. At that time, she was Betty Quinn and we became friends when we started to high school. I do not get to see her today but the imprint she made on my life will never fade. During the time I had my Mother here at home, Betty used to come over to see her Dad, who was in the nursing home here. She would take him riding in the car and they would wind up coming by our house where we could see her Dad and she could see us.

Some time after this, Betty was having trouble remembering some things and she was busy memorizing Scripture while she still could. Looking back, I believe that God was leading her to do this and even today when her memory is unstable, the Scriptures that she learned are such a part of her that they keep her connected to God. What a wonderful Heavenly Father we have! I do not know exactly why the state of our health changes so but I tell myself all the time that God never promised us a life free from all care. Today Betty could not tell me now how it is with her on the inside but I somehow know that God has her in the

6

"palm of His hand!"

To be a child, is a wonderful time of life – a time that is free from the entanglements of grown-up days; a time when our minds are eagerly soaking in all the information that we can find – and a time when we feel that it is our special privilege to make a worth-while contribution to the needs of the people of the world.

Adult-hood sometimes changes many things but the God of our child-hood, is the God of our grown-up days and even promises to be the God of our "golden years."

Psalm 71:17, 18, 20, & 21 (NLT) says – "O God, you have taught me from my earliest childhood, and I have constantly told others about the wonderful things you do. Now that I am old and gray, do not abandon me, O God. Let me proclaim your power to this new generation, your mighty miracles to all who come after me. You have allowed me to suf-fer much hardship, but you will restore me to life again and lift me up from the depths of the earth. You will restore me to even greater honor and comfort me once again."

"Time Waits For No One"

I believe people discuss how fast time comes and goes even more than they discuss the weather. Just this week I have been hearing folks say that the holidays are "right around the corner". It is hard to believe that Thanksgiving is just a couple of weeks away and then Christmas and the beginning of the New Year follow at a close pace.

> "How did it get so late so soon?
> It's night before it's afternoon.
> December is here before it's June.
> My goodness how the time has flown.
> How did it get so late so soon?"
> Dr. Seuss

Dr. Seuss hit the nail on the head. Time ran away for him, also. The

Cat in the Hat tells us that Dr. Seuss knew the value of time and that he illustrated his own convictions by using the talents entrusted to him by God. Most children are familiar with his "Green Eggs and Ham." And, the Cat in the Hat was Dr. Seuss' favorite work. He loved what he did and it shows in what he accomplished.

We should be just as eager to use whatever God has placed within us. And, we really have no time to meander along, trying to think that something good will happen to us without our lifting a finger. I am sure that those of us who are in the late years of life realize that we must capture the moment now. Life is uncertain for us at any age but common sense tells us when we are on the down-side of the hill that we must wisely use what time we have left to make our mark in the world.

God wants to guide us every day in the way we use our time. I do not want to come to the end of life and know that I did not try to live for God. Others may think that what we did was unimportant but only God knows the intent of our hearts. Failure to Him might mean not trying – instead of reaping small results. Whatever our lives amount to is judged by God and His standard is not always the same as ours. Yes, He does look at the value of what we have done but I believe He also takes into consideration just how much we tried.

We are all important to God and each of us has our particular place in this life. I have heard it said that most people would not swap their lives for anyone else's. We are used to living within ourselves and feeling as we do toward what is important to us. Life is certainly wonderful and most of us want to live to a ripe, old age. God says in James 4 vs. 13 – 15 (NLT) – "Look here, you people who say, "Today or tomorrow we are going to a certain town and will stay there a year. We will do business there and make a profit." How do you know what will happen tomorrow? For your life is like the morning fog – it's here a little while, then it's gone. What you ought to say is, "If the Lord wants us to, we will live and do this or that."

Whatever happens, let us decide to do our part in keeping our relationship to God in good repair. Then, we won't have to worry about time because this also will be in God's hands.

"Tell Me the Story of Jesus"

Were we to hear the story of Jesus today for the first time, how would we respond? Would we "drink it all in" or would we listen intently and then walk away?

We are living in the day of vast knowledge that purports many life-styles. What is right for some may not be the right way for us to live. The values of the world are all connected with money and the things that money can buy. God's way is not based on clanking coins or folding money.

Sometimes, we are intellectually and spiritually lazy. It is hard to "think"; to come to some conclusion in our minds as to what life means and what our part in it should be. If we could summarize what we have learned, in the order of its importance, maybe this would be easier for us to follow. My version of the story of Jesus would probably be different from yours. Your perceptions would follow your patterns of thought, coupled with your experiences, and yet the love of God would come through. This is because we are all different and we put the emphasis on things that "speak" to us. But, the most wonderful thing about the differences in your story and mine is the fact that God is so big that He makes your efforts and mine say more than we ever dreamed they could.

If I could put what I believe is the way to live each day of our lives, it might look like an outline for a "how to book." The fact that a relationship has already been established between God and us has to be the basis for any kind of living blessed by God.

The Bible in a nut-shell might be as follows:

John 3:16 – "For God loved the world so much that he gave his only Son so that anyone who believes in him shall not perish but have eternal life."(TLB)

1 John 1:9 – "But if we confess our sins to him, he is faithful and just to forgive us and to cleanse us from every wrong."(NLT)

Philippians 4:6 & 7 – "Don't worry about anything; instead, pray about everything; tell God your needs and don't forget to thank him for his answers. If you do this, you will experience God's peace, which is far more wonderful than the human mind can understand. His peace will keep your thoughts and your hearts quiet and at rest as you trust in Christ Jesus."(TLB)

Proverbs 16:3 – "Commit thy works unto the Lord, and thy thoughts shall be established."(KJV)

Isaiah 26:3 – "Thou wilt keep him in perfect peace, whose mind is stayed on thee: because he trusteth in thee."(KJV)

This is sort of like a blueprint which if we follow will take us through life. From the moment God makes contact with us, He never leaves us. He goes with us through our day by day living forgiving our sins every day and He teaches us to share with Him our daily needs. He wants us to trust Him to supply, not only our actual needs, but His Rx for learning to rest and be quiet. He teaches that the work committed to us is held together in a partnership and we, in turn, commit this work back to Him. We begin to see that the formula for Christian living lies in keeping our mind stayed on God and trusting in Him.

Oh, that we might dare to believe what God tells us! We don't have to rub a magic lamp to get what we want. The source of every blessing lies in the person of Jesus Christ. When we are connected to Him, everything we will ever need is already ours. To follow Jesus is what makes life exciting. We may get lost very easily when we are on an unfamiliar road, but when we consciously follow the Lord, we won't stay lost. God knows every "crook and cranny" of our daily walk and as long as we follow His way, nothing can happen to us that He does not permit. We can travel an unending road that winds up in eternity.

"Shoot For the Moon"

Ever so often, it is good to stop and see just where we are in our lives. When we are young we feel that there is nothing too big for us to do. But, as the years come and go, logic catches up with our infixed dreams that have not come to fruition. This is not to say that those dreams were wrong for us. Maybe our keeping them in the recesses of our hearts

10

helped bring us to today and now helps us take stock of what our real capabilities are. Seeing how brief life is helps us forget the past, concentrate on what is now possible, and gives us a new glimpse of what the future can be.

Everybody has things they want to happen – desires they would like to see come to pass while they are still living. I think this is wonderful. God is so good to us by keeping us "fired up" and looking for the real meaning of life. We show our human side by saying, "I hope to get the farm paid off before I die; or I want to get my degree and be able to teach; or I want to get out of debt before I retire; or may even, I hope to see my grand-children grown up and doing well." We all have dreams and much happiness comes our way when we are busy bringing them into existence.

I was telling Dr. Clarence Wilson, my dentist, what all I would like to do before I pass on and he said, "sounds like another 20 years to me." I don't know when I will be called but maybe the real secret is not in always putting what we want into practice, but tenderly carrying our dreams in our hearts and asking God to cover them with His love. It is good to be needed. God always gives us room to be "what some person needs – in one way or another." And, of course this goes two ways – we need people in our lives to help make us whole.

There is one avenue that we all travel – God needs each of us to be who we are; in whatever way He chooses to use us; and for the length of time that He allows us. He makes no mistakes – His judgments are always past failing.

Someone once said, **"Shoot for the moon. Even if you miss it, you will land among the stars!"**

I am sure that God does not regard failure as we do. When we try, and the results are not what we would like to see, God does not score this as a failure. It might be, in His line of thinking that not daring to try is one form of failure. Also, letting the opinions of others make us uncomfortable when they ridicule our work or ignore it as not meaningful may be part of the meaning of "failure." To be true to God and to the work entrusted to us by Him is our first responsibility. It can and does become our "first" love. Gifts, entrusted to us by our Heavenly Father, are to be shared for the glory of God and the good of others. If we hear a voice

11

that is not audible to everyone, we are to speak up with courage and declare God's message. It is very humbling to be used of God.

Jeremiah 18:1 thru 6(NLT) says "The Lord gave another message to Jeremiah. He said, "Go down to the shop where clay pots and jars are made. I will speak to you while you are there." So I did as he told me and found the potter working at his wheel. But the jar he was making did not turn out as he had hoped, so the potter squashed the jar into a lump of clay and started again. Then the Lord gave me this message, "O Israel, can I not do to you as this potter has done to his clay? As the clay is in the potter's hand, so are you in my hand."

So, whatever happens in our lives, God can fix us!

Let us aim high – if we do not land on the moon, we will still have its light to land on a star!

"Spring Chickens"

When I was a little girl, my Parents used to have a ritual that came about just after spring arrived. They would order "baby chickens" and take them home to grow. I can remember seeing baby chickens, so soft, yellow, and cuddly, at the post office. They were shipped this way and then picked up by the people who ordered them. Their chirping sounds could be heard when we went into the post office to get them.   Their purpose was to be used to provide eggs for us to eat and also delicious fried chicken. Some of them were kept and used to care for other baby chicks that were hatched off later in the year.

The phrase "spring chickens" can be used several ways. I have been told when discussing my age that "you are no spring chicken," meaning that I am climbing the ladder of age. I am learning that this isn't so bad. Every age of our lives has its hard times, but also it's very wonderful times. Youth sees us able to physically do just about anything we need to do, while most of the time, this changes as we age. Some folks have trouble with arthritis while others might never feel this incapacitating pain, but they have to live with other limitations.

This is just the way life is – but, who does not want to live in spite of "what ails us." Whether we are 20 or 70, we want to stay here and live among those we love and who love us. We also are not tired of chasing our dreams and I believe that this is part of what makes life so special. God knows we need something to look forward to; something to participate in so that our day to day living doesn't pick up the drudgery of boredom.

To pay attention to what we might do to help someone else is perhaps the "golden rule" enforced. There is a magic substance that covers us like a heavenly canopy when we give ourselves to others. I know that I barely scratch the surface when I try to live the over-coming life. I want to be able to share what I am, and what I have, while my time is passing here. We come into this world with nothing of material value and our leaving will be the same way. At that time, our clothes won't need pockets because we will be carrying nothing with us.

Hopefully we will already have invested in the riches of heaven. We have done this at every phase of our lives and in every way possible when we lived and loved all who needed us.

Matthew 23:37b (KJV) reads "how often would I have gathered thy children together, even as a hen gathereth her chickens under her wings, and ye would not!" This verse in The New Living Translation says, "How often I have wanted to gather your children together as a hen protects her chicks beneath her wings, but you wouldn't let me!"

Just as a hen gathers and protects her chickens under the shadow of her wings, God covers and protects us. We can trust Him just as the chickens trust the hen to be their strength and sufficiency. We trust God by trusting His Word which provides all the defense we will ever need – whatever the circumstances.

"Today Is All the Time We Have"

The clock is continually ticking! Seconds turn into minutes and minutes into hours. The beginning of the day turns into the ending of the day and today becomes "yesterday."

Everyone has memories of days gone by - some are good and we relish them; others are not so good but we remember that the Lord has forgiven and forgotten our sin. That is, if we have asked for His forgiveness. 1 John 1:9 says this – "But if we confess our sins to him, he is faithful and just to forgive us and cleanse us from every wrong."

I believe most people are sincere about living a Christian life. Because I know myself, I can see that every thing I do is not perfect and the same goes for most others. It is so easy to put off until tomorrow something we should do today. Tomorrow may never come for us because no one knows the length of his (or her) life.

So, in light of how fast time goes by and how unsure we are as to the length of our days here, how do we cope day by day? For me, because I am attached to the Creator of the world, I can swing around on one foot; pivot for balance, and not fall because my position as God's child ensures complete safety. This is true for everyone.

But, just being safe – (as wonderful as this is) – is not enough to make us happy. There has to be something that we can pour our soul's desire into that is bigger than we are. And, perhaps this is the answer – God says in Jeremiah 1:5 "I knew you before I formed you in your mother's womb. Before you were born I set you apart and appointed you as my spokesman to the world."

Our individual lives are different. God wants us to be happy and whatever we need, He knows, because He made us. Families are very important and one of God's sweetest gifts. We need a place of our own – a place where we can be refueled for every day's living. The older I get the more I believe that life does not have to be a daily battle-ground but a hallowed particle of time where God fights and wins our battles. He sets us up under a huge umbrella where the sun's rays fall around its perimeter. He beds us down on the banks of a stream of sweet-flowing, cold water. And He covers us for the night's rest with His mantle of love. What more could we need? This is the kind of life for which we were made.

As we catch a vision of who we were destined to be and what we were destined to do, we find it easier to forget yesterday and not to worry about tomorrow. Providing we have a tomorrow, it can be a repeat of today – only better. This walk with God is tied up in a personal relationship and we can surely count on Him to never change in His love for us. God is never wishy- washy and we can trust Him with our whole weight.

Whether we are young, old, or in-between, the gauntlet has been passed to us. What we do with the challenge of God makes up our lives. There is no retirement from God's call. In fact, it is what provides us with strength to go on living when sorrow comes. It calls forth from our inner beings laughter and a sweet spirit of love and contentment. And, this call can bind up our wounds (regardless of their origin). The call of God to each of His children encases us in a sphere of sweet-smelling perfume. This aroma from heaven, given and used by God's Spirit, calls out to those who need the Lord and helps them come to Him. This is Life's Greatest Purpose!

"We Only Live Once"

"Only one life, 'twill soon be past,
Only what's done for Christ will last!"
(Author Unknown)

I found these words long ago written on a book-mark. I think I still have it somewhere around here. The paper it is written on may be wrinkled and old but the words are ever new!

When I was younger, I did not realize how quickly time passes and how soon we would be caught up in the middle years of our lives, and even in the "golden years," Time goes by fast and our day by day living brings changes all the time. Youth is the ideal time to pledge our allegiance to God and to begin the journey across the span of time. We are all on the "march" and I do not think that God views our wandering in the wilderness as completely lost time. He can take the minutest attention that we give Him and make it worth-while. It would be wonderful if we could just go immediately to being the kind of person that God wants us to be. But, it doesn't happen this way. Just as a pearl is fashioned by the daily grinding of sand and water, our characters are formed as God allows the rough edges of life to change us. The story of the frog in the churn of cream can be our way out of any situation – we come to ourselves; we begin to paddle in the churn that has us trapped; and slowly rise on the butter until we can hop out to freedom.

To consider what makes our actions as something that is done for Christ gets to be quite complicated. We know that God views anything that we do for someone else just like we were doing it for Him – even sharing a cup of cold water. This can apply to anything that benefits others. When we think of something as being small and insignificant, we are missing the point. Nothing is worthless to God and anything that makes some one's suffering less is considered His work. When we permit God to lead in the daily living of our lives, many things will open up during the day that would not be possible for us without Him. Our vision may be short-sighted and we may not be able to see the opportunities of the day because we cannot see that far.

I think that any of us can learn to live for God – that is, if we really want to. Sometimes, our "want-to" has to have surgical procedures. God can remove our love for what is not to our best advantage and He can fire-up our interest and love for Him. Life is wonderful and God wants us to find this to be true!

Regardless of our age, we never get too old to begin to do something for God. The world does not run just by the big, explosive happenings of life, but by the small ways we live every day to show that life is good and that God loves each of us. Every so called "small" overture we extend to someone else not only makes that person's life better but it helps to distribute God's concern for everyone. We, as God's children, are helping to "hold the sky in place" and give God more opportunity to reach others before their lives are over. We are already on the side of good and every time we feel the refreshing Presence of God, we know that we really belong to Him. We don't have to be perfect people to walk with God every day and to know that He is with us every day and night of our lives.

Trying to make every day of our lives count for "good" is the only way to happiness here and it leads to the joy of being with Our Heavenly Father when this life is over. Living for God is sort of like trying to learn how to do anything new – it looks so complicated and impossible that we are afraid to try. But, regardless of how hard something new looks to be, when we get involved in it, the pieces begin to fall together.

16

We don't learn to use a computer in a moment. Jane Medlin taught me all I know about my computer. She used to explain things to me and I could not quite understand all the connections. She said that one day, it would all fall in place and I would be able to work without so much assistance from her. This happened and I will always be thankful for her help. (Just don't tell her that I don't know everything yet).

Only one life, yes only one! God never gets tired of teaching us. He says in Philippians 1 vs. 6 (The Living Bible) "And I am sure that God who began the good work within you will keep right on helping you grow in his grace until his task within you is finally finished on that day when Jesus Christ returns."

"Take Off Your Shoes, For This Is Holy Ground"

There is enough wisdom in the Book of Joshua to carry us through a lifetime – regardless of what we are called on to experience. Joshua served as Moses right-hand man and traveled with the children of Israel as they made their way out of Egypt. He witnessed the leading of God as the moon gave them light; he ate the manna from Heaven as his daily food; and he drank from the rock that Moses inadvertently struck in his frustration. God's commands are highly visible in the life of Moses. After Moses died, Joshua was appointed by God to be the leader of this group of Israelites.

In their travels, the people camped on the plains of Moab as God gave instructions to Joshua as to how he was to get the people across the Jordan River. Earlier, Joshua had seen how God had dried up the waters of the Red Sea, permitting the people to walk across on dry land. He was told by God that this miracle was about to be repeated; that the waters of the Jordan would be drawn back and that the river-bed would be dried up where the people could walk across on dry land. After all this had materialized, and the people were safely across, the water flowed again and overflowed the banks as it had before.

I'm sure that Joshua remembered that God said He would be with him as He had been with Moses. God performed these miracles so that the nations of the earth might know the power of the Lord and might learn to fear Him as their God forever.

Joshua lived to be 110 years of age but perhaps one of the most significant things he learned during his lifetime of service to God happened when he encountered the commander of the Lord's army. This transpired one day when he came face-to-face with a man armed with a sword. Joshua went up to him and asked, "Are you friend or foe?" The man replied, "Neither one. I am commander of the Lord's army." At this, Joshua fell with his face to the ground in reverence, "I am at your command," Joshua said. "What do you want your servant to do?" The commander of the Lord's army replied, "Take off your sandals, for this is holy ground." And Joshua did as he was told. Joshua 5:13-15, (NLT).

If we but open our eyes, we will know that many times we are "standing on holy ground." The only stability that life has to offer is when we stand on the promises of God and trust Him to take care of us. Joshua served God his entire life and this is our highest privilege, also. When our lives are over, the only eulogy we will need is one that says God was with us all the way and that the sum total of life was spent "standing on holy ground." All life is sacred! God made the world and everything in it! Nature shows the beauty that is hidden in God. Our animal companions show us aspects of God's love when they stay close to us and show their individual personalities. And people – we couldn't get along without our families and friends.

Hopefully we can learn to realize that experiencing life itself is an indicator that we are "standing on holy ground!"

"The Trackless Heavens"

There is a meeting place in the sky where our prayers come in contact with the God of the Universe!

This is the way it seems to me – as soon as our hearts send prayers to God, they are set loose from us and balloon out into the vast area of blue and white clouds; sun and shadows, rain and gentle breezes. The words

18

that were audible upon leaving us become hidden in the mysteries of God's world and are parachuted into His Presence. Perhaps they are born upon the wings of angels and the melody of these wings in flight send our prayers to the feet of Jesus.

I am convinced that all of heaven's inhabitants move to love and please God. There are no maps to help us find our way except for the words found in the Bible. No road signs as we have them here point to the Lord. There are no tracks to follow except those set by others who have gone before us. Perhaps the routes that migrating birds use are secondary roads way below the paths set in fog and invisible to the human eye.

This is a good time to think of how powerful God is and how so much above us are His attributes. We were made to have communion with God but have you ever really thought of how amazing this is? Some day we will move into our heavenly home but even now, we are not just "marking time", we are living our lives here under His guidance. And, from time to time, He permits us to catch a glimpse of that something that we call "eternity". My mind gets all cloudy when I try to think of something that never ends. And, this is exactly what we are promised!

We need to make sure that our relationship with God is right. I can remember one time when I did not know if I would live or die and how compelling was the thought – "am I all right with God?" I had to stop and pray, asking that God forgive me if there was anything wrong in my life. When the "chips are down", this is our most important question – "am I all right with God."

I find that I have to pray this prayer many times to keep things on an even keel with Him. This cleansing that God grants to us guarantees that one day we will have safe passage through the trackless skies and even now, it is the main requisite of peace and companionship with our Heavenly Father.

I never tire of the way God answers prayer. As I pray about something, I would like God to explain to me just what He is going to do and how He is going to do it. But, the answer never comes this way. Perhaps, this would supercede the way of 'faith' were God to do this. But, when I begin to look for new ways to view my problem and strength to accept it for what it is, I sometimes find answers that help me to "keep on , keeping on." I have learned that God can chisel down my problem to my size and can give me renewed confidence that everything is going to be all right. He can multiply the hours that I have allowed for a certain project, and help me complete my work on time. These are not new ideas, but, we need to be reminded again and again that God can always help us more. He makes us see with new clarity that life is good; that people are wonderful; and that we are even now living on the outskirts of the "trackless heavens."

"The Lord is my strength and my song, he has become my victory." Psalm 118:14 NLT

"Live Every Day as if it were Your Last"

"Live every day as if it were your last, because one of these days, it will be." This saying was written by author, Jeremy Schwartz, who is known for his famous quotes.

I'm sure it would be quite a blow to visit our physician and learn that something was wrong with our body; something serious, and life-threatening. As he would explain all our options to us, our mind and our emotions might run and jump with fear causing quite a time of upheaval. We would have to calm down and do the proper thing of deciding what method of healing we would follow.

There could be times when the doctor would tell us that we only have a certain number of days to live and his diagnosis could be wrong. The story is told that Walter Matthau, one of our finest actors, said this, "My doctor gave me six months to live, but when I couldn't pay the bill he gave me six months more." This is supposed to help lighten our thinking but truly, the time limit on our lives is classified information and only God has the password to His program. I am so glad that only He decides when my last day to live will be.

Some folks might react to this startling news by throwing "all caution to the winds." They sometimes decide to just put all of this bad news out of mind and live each day as though they were going to live forever. The book of Isaiah – chapter 22, verses 8 thru 14, (The Living Bible)

tells what happens to us when God removes his protecting care. We can manage our plans to escape all our misery, never calling on God for help and nothing will work out for us. God wants us to change our way of thinking and living and turn to Him. But, some will refuse to change their way. They will say, "Let us eat, drink, and be merry. What's the difference, for tomorrow we die?"

This is a terrible delimina in which to be. When we fail to meet God's terms, we cut off our only hope of safety. Some of Jesus' followers went back believing that His words were too hard to follow. When Jesus asked the twelve disciples if they, too, were going to go away, Simon Peter said, "Lord, to whom shall we go? Thou hast the words of eternal life". John 6 v 68 (KJV).

It is a very dangerous thing to turn our back on Jesus – life is uncertain and if we wait, we might not have another opportunity to make things right with Him. However long we live in this world, and whatever material things we might enjoy; it is all a rip-off if we fail to get into Heaven where we will live with God forever and ever! There we will have the things to enjoy that God has prepared for us all. I Corinthians 2 v 9 (KJV) reads "But as it is written, Eye hath not seen, nor ear heard, neither have entered into the heart of man, the things which God hath prepared for them that love him." At the same time, we will be safe from every evil influence that exists.

I am not afraid of what will happen to me after I die. I guess my concern is with how everything might have to be worked out before I die. I am a "chicken" and I have asked God many times to sort of slip my day of departure up on me. I know that He will work everything out just right – not only the day, but everything connected with it. I saw so many of my people die last year, and I was amazed at the way God took care of all of them. He is so merciful and knowledgeable and I trust Him to give me an extra portion of His grace when my time comes. Someone once told me that God will give us "dying grace" when the time comes and I believe He does enable us to make this transition in a way that is pleasing to Him. I am convinced when I take care of today and do the best I can to live for God, He will take care of me and whatever the day might hold, He will be more than able to see me thru it.

"There Are Some Things Money Can't Buy"

Buy now – pay later! This is the way many people use their buying power these days.

For those of us who do not have a lot of money, this way of living helps us get some of the things we need quicker than we could were we to wait and save up the entire purchase price. Quick credit has its drawbacks, though. If we are not careful, we can find ourselves in debt up to our necks. And, it is harder to pay off our accounts than it is to charge in the first place.

MasterCard says – "there are some things money can't buy. For everything else there's MasterCard."

Wouldn't it be nice if we could just whip out our credit card, charge our items, and never have to worry about paying the balance? But, we know business does not operate this way. Interest is added to the purchase price and this can make what we buy cost several times what it should.

There are some real things money can't buy. God has His own monetary system. He doesn't have to worry about copper pennies, new half-dollars, or printing new paper money. His storehouse is filled with walls of kindness; floors of concern for our neighbor; and the roof is etched with the golden glow of love. We do not write checks on this account. We automatically have everything we need because we belong to God.

We can have whatever we need – today. As long as our hearts are in tune with our Heavenly Father, our signature is all we need. No co-signer is necessary – these transactions are just between God and us. Delivery of what we need may not be immediate. God may have to deliver our shipment along with a shipment to our neighbor, friend, or family. But, we are guaranteed sure delivery. His guarantee is written and signed in blood and we can expect delivery of our purchase in God's time. It won't be early, or late, and it may be carried by the "brown truck" or by a representative of the foot patrol.

We do not have a credit limit – we may have all that our faith can appropriate. There are no finance charges, no shipping charges. Our Heavenly Father offers "eternal life, peace that passes all understanding, great joy in our hearts, and most of all, all the love we need." The card He gives us will never expire, never go out-of-date and its possession will fill us with such a measure of hope that our every day here can be "a new beginning." Just knowing that all our needs are being met today and being confident that God has taken care of the future is priceless knowledge.

Yes, there are some things money can't buy. There are some things even MasterCard can't cover but in God's scheme of things, purchases have already been made for us. All we need do is "receive." I am sure that even after a lifetime, we have just barely "scratched the surface" when considering God and His ways.

Once in awhile, we are permitted to catch a glimpse of some inner knowledge that has no name for us – yet. This is a blessing that whets the appetite for "more." These are "mountain-top" times for us. But, let us remember that the bedrock of our faith lies in the words found in Romans 10:9 (TLB) "For if you tell others with your own mouth that Jesus Christ is your Lord, and believe in your own heart that God has raised him from the dead, you will be saved." Eternal life is priceless – without the confidence that heaven will be our home when we die, the baubles of this life would not suffice and boredom would be our constant companion. We can burst open the shells of indifference and make our lives just as exciting as we dare!

"Is Your Cup Half-Empty or Half-Full?"

How full our cup is depends on how we look at life. Some of us have been conditioned during our lives to take the gloomy outlook and see that our cup is already half-empty. This is not the ideal way to view any situation. Some folks can look at a cup where the ingredients have been used up part of the way and see a cup that is still half-full.

It is not good to see only what is gone – we need to appreciate what is left. This can be applied to so many different things in our lives. Most of the time when we are very young, we accept the cup as it is and do not analyze the size of its contents. But, as we get older, we find ourselves being swayed from "half-full to half-empty."

Nothing in our lives stays the same forever. Graduation from high school brings lots of changes – school as we knew it here is over and some things we loved so much must be left behind. This frees us up where we can embrace new things and learn to live with a new direction. This is part of growing-up and this letting go of the old and picking up the new is a routine that will be repeated throughout the rest of our lives.

As we age, we become less agile and more careful; we become less tight-fisted and more accepting of change; and we become less geared to strange ideas and more secure in our relationship with God. We appreciate what we can do now – physically and mentally, and we do not try to hang on to the way we used to be when we were very young. We remember to look at someone else's situation and see how fortunate we really are. We tell God over and over how much we love Him and how we thank Him for people to love and for those who love us. Even our animals become extra-special because they fill a void in our lives and they show their love for us in their own way. They climb on our chair; they sleep on any piece of clothing that we fail to hang up; and they rub around our feet – just to show they care. Every inch of love that we experience is just an extension of God's love for us and His world.

My cup is half-full when I think of my home. Some folks do not have a home and I love the one God provided for my Mother and me. It is so nice to enter the living-room and be out of the extremes of the weather. A good, clean bed is a blessing, and so are nice, clean clothes to wear. Water to be used for drinking and bathing, etc. is such a wonderful thing. Some folks in the world have no home, no bed, and no clean water. I do not want to ever forget to thank God for all the things that make up our daily lives. We are rich beyond measure! Foods, automobiles, money to pay our utilities, are some of the things we could take for granted.

Not long ago, someone told me that she is unable to do much of her work around the house. But, she said as long as she could get up, take care of her own physical needs and not have to ask anyone for help, that she is doing fine. So many people cannot even get out bed without help, and have to be dressed and fed. My niece, Linda lives at the Caruthersville Nursing Center and she is completely dependent on others. She goes to Church on Sunday afternoon out there and loves going. She told me today that she would pray for me because I had been sick. I think she has

24

learned this since she has been going to church out there.

Yes, if we realistically look at our lives today, we have to come to the conclusion that our cup is always "half-full" and that much of the time, it is "running-over" because God is so good to us!

"The earth is full of the goodness of the Lord." Psalm 33:5b (KJV)

"We Will Always Remember"

The year of 2001 will always be prefaced with the notation of the terrible acts of September 11th. These things that happened were so vile, so brutal, and so unrealistic that they could never be understood. We were forced to accept the consequences of these actions because there was no other way out. We can't undo what has already been done. Thousands of people would have given their own lives to change the course of events that took place on that day.

Many scholars have thought about the question why do bad things happen to good people . I certainly do not have all the answers as to "why" bad things happen to us. I can quote Psalm 46 vs. 1 (KJV) - "God is our refuge and strength, a very present help in trouble." All I know how to do is hang on to the hand of God – believing that He is aware of every danger and that He will protect me now and also when the next attack comes. Some things are so big that only God has the real answers. I don't think He minds our trying to understand when these things happen but He knows that ultimately we will have to leave them in His hands.

 I have been doing quite a bit of thinking lately about the uncertainty of life and all the things that can happen to us as we grow older.   Last week in Church, this came to my mind – I was impressed to realize that I do not have to understand all the "ins-and-outs" of life. God will take care of us in the future – just as He does now – a day at a time. My Mother told me when she and my Father had small children (before I came along) and one of the children would get sick, my Dad would have her go to bed with the children and he would sit beside the bed with his leg propped up on the bed. When someone moved, he would wake up and be ready to help in any way needed. I like to think that God is always sitting "beside our bed" ready to take any action needed to take care of us.

There is another angle to this scenario and it is <u>what to do when bad things happen to good people</u>. It is a certainty that each of us will experience some form of grief and sorrow that come from bad things happening. Our lives quite naturally bump up against some form of unrest. Sometimes bad things happen when we get out of doing what we know is right. There is a price we pay for not following God's instructions. He doesn't want to hurt us but He is very concerned with our getting back on the right terms with Him. Many times the forces of evil will take "pot shots" at us. God tells us in Ephesians 6 vs. 11 (KJV) – "Put on the whole armour of God, that ye may be able to stand against the wiles of the devil."

God knows what happened here September 11, 2001. He knows what He expects of our country in view of what the correct criteria should be for us. The pros and cons of how we should defend ourselves and how we should view our status in the world are matters that we must leave to the proper channels. All I know is that God knows about the fall of every person and He sees the brokenness of every heart that has suffered loss. He will always remember this day – as will we!

———————

"Life Has Many Beginnings and Many Endings"

It would be almost impossible to jot down all the ways our lives begin and end from the day of our birth to the day of our death. We have always heard it said that two things in life are certain – those being taxes and death. My Mother used to tell me that we start dying from the day we are born.

Life here begins when we leave the warmth and safety of our Mother's womb and make our entrance into this world. But, this is not the end for us – it is only the beginning. With the aid of our parents, we try to learn how to find our place in the family structure; in school functions;

and in ways to make our lives useful in alleviating the hurts of the world. I think some people are born with this need to help others. Some folks find their soul-mates and begin families of their own. This gives them additional work to do because they must show their children what they have found to be true thus far in their lives. What a privilege to share in your children's hopes and dreams for the future.

Some of us never find this kind of life and must try to find other ways to make our lives just as real and just as happy. The meaning of life is not confined to one avenue – there are as many ways to live meaningful lives as there are people. We are all individuals and God has made each of us different from anyone else. One big day in the life of a working person is the day of retirement. This, too, is not the end for us – it is only the beginning. I don't believe God ever lets us just "sit and rock on the front porch of life." Under His direction, we can now find time to try new things and perhaps discover that we have found the real joy of our lives.

Everything we learn, from the day we are born thru the length of all our lives here, can be stepping-stones when used to enrich someone else's life. God made us want to live; to hold on to this thing called life, and to make it "good" with all of our ability. There is much we do not know about death but when we look through the eyes of faith, we can believe that this, too, is not the end for us – it is only the beginning!

I sometimes wonder how God spends His day – what is His schedule. And, then I remember that Life there is not like it is here. I don't believe they have time clocks, schedules to keep as we do, and hurdles to climb to find peace. But, I do believe that when we leave this world, we carry all that we are with us. Our interests here may be magnified there. You, who have the loving hearts of mothers and fathers, may find others who need you when that day comes. Teachers may find those who need to be taught to recognize what they have inherited. Doctors will be out of business because there will be no sickness in Heaven but their knowledge may be utilized in other ways. Who knows – Heaven may have a newspaper and I may be permitted to write a column for it. Our Pastors may be used to lead as shepherds under the tutorage of "The Great Shepherd" and they may help us not to get lost. Our Choirs may join in with the heavenly singing and those who are proficient in playing instruments may get to play on the harps of Heaven. I am not trying to write a story – my point is "all things are possible when we get up there." Perhaps what gives us the most joy now may be ours to keep when we make the transition. And, however God chooses to fulfill our needs and desires, it will be just right! Because He says in I Corinthians 2 vs. 9, (KJV) – "But as it is written, Eye hath not seen, nor ear heard, neither have entered into the heart of man, the things which God hath prepared for them that love him."

"I'll Always Love You"

Back in 1989 the children's book, "I'll Always Love You" first appeared in print. It was written by Hans Wilhelm and soon had the distinction of being classified by the Kansas City Star as a classic in children's literature.

The narrator is a young boy and the story is about Elfie, a dachshund, – "the best dog in the whole world." From the time Elfie is a puppy, she and the boy are together daily. When she is young, Elfie is full of pep and pranks; but as her master grows taller and taller, Elfie grows fatter and slower. One morning, Elfie does not wake up. The boy and his whole family grieve and they bury their beloved pet. Though someone offers the boy a new puppy, he refuses because he knows that he is not ready for a new pet. But, when he is ready for a new friend, he will tell that one, as he told Elfie every night, "I'll always love you."
This is an important message for children as well as adults. Every living thing has to die – every goldfish, every cat, every bird, even every flower that blooms. This is something that is hard for children to understand. And, really, is there anyone, regardless of age or background, who understands all that makes up this experience?

This story tries to teach, not only the fact that everyone and everything dies, but also that we need to take advantage of our opportunities to express our love – not only to people that we love, but also to our pets who are our daily companions. It is a fact that love really does "beget" love. It is impossible to love someone without it affecting how they feel toward us. We do not love primarily so someone will love us back. Real love is loving, whether it is returned or not. But, we always hope for a mutual exchange.

It is always good to tell others how we feel. Some families are quite open in expressing their love. Others are hesitant to openly declare how they feel. Part of our make-up now is determined by how affection was expressed when we were growing up. My Mother never found it easy to tell me that she loved me but I never doubted her love. She showed it in so many ways. So, it was hard for me to say the things I wanted to say to her. But, after she got sick, it was my privilege to tell her every day that I loved her. And, part of these ten years that she was sick, I know she understood what I was saying. Really, who knows how much a person understands even when we think they do not know. We should express our love anyway and it is entirely possible that it finds a listening ear in our loved one.

I am an animal lover! I can certainly identify with others who have lost their beloved pets. My niece, Linda Burnett, gave me a little medallion one time that I carry in my car. It reads –"guardian angel of cats" and I am this; but, in addition, I find myself looking out for dogs, birds or anything that is alive. Mary Alice Roberts, who lives a few blocks down from me, has a beautiful, white duck that I love to see waddle across her yard. Bill Morgan has a black dog and a brown dog that I always look for when I go by his house. They may be part Labradors; I am not sure. This is part of being alive for me – to co-exist with animals. My cats here, if they could, would surely tell you how I tell each of them that I love them. And, I know they love me too!

God loved us so much that He gave His only Son that we might be reconciled to Him. (John 3:16). Love is kept alive in the world today because God infuses our hearts with His love. I John 4:16 (KJV) reads – "And we have known and believed the love that God hath to us. God is love; and he that dwelleth in love dwelleth in God and God in him."

God tells us, "I'll always love you" and we pick up the gauntlet by saying the same thing to those we love!

"God Cares For Us"

1st Peter 5:7 tells us exactly what we are to do; why we are to do it; and indicates what the situation will be when this is accomplished.

The New Living Translation tells us –"Give all your worries and cares to God, for he cares about what happens to you." The Living Bible says – "Let him have all your worries and cares, for he is always thinking about you and watching everything that concerns you." The King James Version simply says – "casting all your care upon him; for he careth for you."

To begin with, we have been told over and over again that God loves us. This was probably the thing that most attracted us to Him when we first started our spiritual journey. However; wherever; and whenever the point of contact was made – the moment came when we actively took God into our lives – and He took us into His. I can remember long ago, one night on my knees, the bond between God and me was fixed. There was no music, no spoken words from God but I found something within me that here-to-fore had lain dormant. I did not receive a telephone call from God but I found that the Bible is full of letters that I needed to read. They were more important to me than any piece of mail sent by "priority mail" and God honored my feeble efforts, as He does for everyone who seeks Him. There were times I wondered if everything was clear between God and me. Someone older and wiser than me advised me to go through the same process that I had engaged in many moons ago. I sought the Lord again and He made our transaction valid. This was something I had to learn for myself.

I'd like to say that every day after this, I lived a glowing Christian life but I had my days of failure and disappointment. God did not take me off His list when I fouled up. He never disowned me as His child. He began to teach me to "give him all my troubles and cares" and assured me that He still cared for me. I sort of began to understand that when we were told to give Him these dark and immature parts of us that He knew exactly what to do with them. My problems were just beginning. I had to learn that He expects me to let Him do the leading.

It is so satisfying to know that someone is thinking about us and watching over everything that concerns us. God's table of weights and measures is quite different from ours. When we are ignored or passed over for a moment of recognition, God has a way of making us see that this is not so important anyway. To have the inner knowledge that God is working in us; for us; and through us is probably one of life's greatest blessings.

Casting our care on Him is not a one-time thing – we usually find that life has a way of making this action necessary quite often. So many things in life are set up on this scale – we find that the need to tell our loved ones how we feel is something that seems to come more often day by day. And, the need to be told that we are loved is not a one-time thing; Yesterday's gentleness does not make today's needs less. The way we turn loose of our worries and cares is something that we probably have in common; and yet, we each have to learn to do this for ourselves. We want this transaction between God and us to be freeing to our personalities. For this to be the way it should be, we must come to Him and be quite open about everything. God already knows all about us. But, when He gets a free rein to work in our lives, He erases what is not pleasing to Him and causes us to walk so tall that it looks like we are walking on "stilts." There is no room here for us to be egotistical; we only walk this way because He cares for us!

"I Saw an Angel"

One morning when I had been driving in the cemetery, I looked down the exit drive and saw a full-sized figure standing near a marker. I wondered what he was doing. He was standing erect and perfectly still. I decided to investigate and when I got nearly there, I realized that it was not a man, but the statue of an angel. I thought of the many times I had driven by that spot and had never this angel.

I got out of the car and looked at the tombstone located at the head of the grave. It was the figure of a beautifully carved angel with distinct facial features and marked hands and fingers. The shoulders had a covering of a robe-like garment that extended the entire length of the body. It was standing over the grave of a person who had died in 1920. I'm sure the color of the stone statue was originally white but the residue from the trees near-by had painted it shades of black and gray with a hint of blue. It was still very beautiful!

Probably the family had this angel placed, standing over their loved one, as a symbol of God's protection. It is inspiring to know that many people do somehow believe that God sends angels to help us during our lives here. It is a beautiful thing to fill our minds with the knowledge that God always helps us and many times He sends His Angels from Heaven to do His bidding. The main point of this story is not that "I saw an angel" but in reality that God reinforced in my mind that He is always on the look-out for us. God does take care of us and sometimes He does it with the aid of His angels.

I ran several references in the Bible on "angels." They are definitely a part of God's creation. Many verses tell of their "talking and flying" as they engaged in doing God's will. Psalm 77 says that the bread from heaven that God sent down to the children of Israel when they were in the wilderness was actually "the food of angels." I do not believe that God's attention to us covers us automatically without any participation on our part. Our inheritance does not come just because we are living and part of the human race. God woos us, wanting our love and trust in Him to be real. He mentions in Psalm 78:39 that "we are mortal and that we are gone in a moment like a breath of wind, never to return." Eternity is forever and cannot compare with time as we know it now. We need to make provision for the end of life because it is just the beginning of our eternal destiny.

Angels are so wonderfully and beautifully made. One of my friends told me about her husband who had a visit from an angel. He was living his last days here and he told her that someone came to his room in the night and said, "be not afraid!" Only God has the words of eternal life and He is the one we need to lead us as we go through our days here. He has promised that He will take care of us when this life is over. He will not; He cannot let us down!

Dr. Norman Vincent Peale told a story about an experience that a man had while out walking in the woods. He was alone but he kept hearing voices. After looking all around, and seeing no one; He glanced up and saw a group of angels flying over-head. They were in conversation with each other and paid no attention to him. He could not understand what was being said but he heard their voices until they were completely out of sight. I respected Dr. Peale and if he said this happened, I believe that it did. Just because we have not experienced something ourselves does not mean that it could not happen.

I have never seen a real angel but this does not mean that they do not exist or that others may not have seen them. I have been aware of their presence with me and feel confident that their protection has helped me

many times. I believe with all my heart what is said in Ps. 91:11(KJV) –
"For he shall give his angels charge over thee, to keep thee in all thy
ways." To be connected to God is life's highest calling and one that is
available to every living person!

"Have You Hugged Your Cat Today?"

No animal lover would think that this is a foolish question. They might
think it would be more fitting if we were talking about a dog. Some
folks like birds, fish and a few other things that even I think are weird ,
like snakes and skunks. But, many people in the world love animals and
have them in their homes.

One of my sisters used to tell me "don't kiss that cat." She thought this
was a little too much and maybe it is for some people. When we have
animals that belong to us, it is our duty and privilege to take care of
them. It gets to be pretty expensive buying food and medicine, and
helping them get their shots and other kinds of care from the vet.
Anytime I go to Wal-mart, I see a lot of people buying cat food, etc.,
and some of them are men and young people, as well as "little, old
ladies."

My cats always seem to need fresh water; their food bowls get empty
and they follow me every where I go in the house, rubbing against my
legs and trying to tell me to notice them. When Gracie Le was very
young, she would follow me all the time. When my Mother was here,
I would get up in the middle of the night to give her medicine and turn
her in bed, and when I was in the kitchen fixing the medicine, I would
feel this ball of fir rubbing against my feet and Gracie Le would be beg-
ging for attention. Gracie always slept on my bed and she knew when I
got up.

We are fortunate to have Dr. Bill Dickerson for our vet. He is such an
animal lover and a very fine Christian man as well. I am sure that he
has found the work that God placed him here to do. Mrs. Dickerson is
in a Christian vocation as well and they are raising their children in this
kind of loving atmosphere.

My cats have their own way of knowing when I am upset or very tired. They love to stand on their hind legs, and reach up to me with their front paws. They seem to be saying, "can I help you?" They sleep in my favorite chair and perch on the arms when I sit down to rest. Many times when I fall asleep, they fall asleep also, and are still there when I awake.

My life would surely be empty without my cats. I John 4 vs. 8 (The Living Bible) says "But if a person isn't loving and kind, it shows that he doesn't know God – for God is love." This surely does away with the idea that we have the right to abuse anyone or anything. Animals were created by God; they have their rightful place in our world; and this dispels the theory that any kind of animal abuse is legitimate. I believe God abhors ill treatment of people and animals.

My four cats – Billy Boy, Calico, Baby Gray, and Gracie Le all know that I love them and it is my joy to hug each of them every day!

"Goodness and Mercy are Our Constant Companions"

As individuals, we each have our own set of physical features that allow other people to know who we are. I may be old, you may be young; I may have gray hair, you may have color on your hair; and I may have difficulty walking, while you may be as spry as a "spring chicken."

But, there is another side of us that cannot be seen. No one can see under the skin where the heart is beating, the lungs are breathing, and the blood is flowing through the arteries to every part of our bodies. These are the areas that our doctor has to try and investigate. He may use a ct scan and even injections of nuclear medicine to try to diagnose our ailments. This is one way that God heals today. Our doctor uses information passed on to him through the goodness of God even to knowing what kind of prescription to give us. All of this "knowing what to do for us and what medicine to give us" surely comes from a God who can identify with our infirmities. It may be that we have not arrived at the place where we can believe that Jesus still heals folks today. But, most of us can look back and see periods of sickness that we were brought through and we know that only God could have made our illnesses go away.

If a light could be put on our inward parts, deeper reaching than x-rays, we might just get an inkling of what makes us "who we are." The song, "Me and My Shadow" is probably more descriptive than we know. There is a part of us that cannot be reached by human means. It has been said that regardless of how far we travel, or how fast, we cannot get away from ourselves. We have to take who we are with us. The irony of this is that by the time we grow up, we are in the process of learning to love ourselves and we do not feel the need to leave ourselves at home.

God never classifies us as "hopeless or useless." If we can look back, we will be able to see that what we want out of life is different from what we used to want. This plateau of spiritual development has been reached only through the goodness and mercy of God. This is not boasting knowledge, but it brings to us a deep satisfaction when we can see that God is our Partner and that without Him in our lives, we would be just as mixed-up as we used to be.

We can take life as it comes because we now believe and know that "goodness and mercy are our constant companions." God will never let anything touch us that He has not willed, or permitted. The Promise found in Psalm 23:6 is ours to claim and to use continually. This promise never loses its power to help us regardless of the times it has been put to the test. What we need today are Bible-believing Christians, ready and willing to put to the test every promise that we have been given. God will always honor such a commitment. I want to be this kind of Christian, don't you?

"Your goodness and unfailing kindness shall be with me all my life, and afterwards I will live with you forever in your home." Psalm 23:6 (The Living Bible).

Most of us are more familiar with the King James Version which says – "Surely goodness and mercy shall follow me all the days of my life: and I will dwell in the house of the Lord for ever."

"This Is Your Life"

This is a phrase that was used on a television show some years ago. Ralph Edwards was the host and the show was built around events that had happened in the guest's life. It is always interesting to see how others have lived their lives.

Back in the 1800's, there lived a man who was not afraid to be a loaner. He was not a social misfit because he had many friends but he was a person who dared to be himself. Henry David Thoreau, (1817-1862), only lived forty-five years but he managed to make an imprint on many folks then and his work is still here today having survived many years of scrutiny.

Thoreau withdrew from mainstream society; built himself a cabin on the shores of Walden Pond and lived there two years partaking of his first love – "nature." He occupied himself with basic needs and sought to be free of the hurry and anxiety of those who lived in a hurry-scurry way.

In comparing our lives with his, we live in a world that is totally different from that of the early and middle 1800's. It is up to us to make what we can of our lives. It is vital that we have our own individual "work" and I believe that this is where our "talents" come in as God helps us make our lives count for good. How to avoid letting this rush-about way of living engulf us is a goal that we must work toward. It is easy to see that we do not have all the answers regarding just how we are to live.

Thoreau did much thinking as he pondered the world and his place in it. He said, "Go confidently in the direction of your dreams. Live the life you have imagined." We should be so thankful for our dreams. God has honored us by placing in our minds and hearts some of His goals for us.

We need to give free rein to everyone – to let them be what they can be, not what is necessarily expected of them. Thoreau knew about this too. He wrote, "If a man does not keep pace with his companions, perhaps it is because he hears a different drummer. Let him step to the music which he hears, however measured or far away." This honors the diversity of personalities which God ordained long ago.

Every day we are here, our lives grow shorter. This is a fact that is noted – not to cause us to be in a frenzy – but to show us the sacredness of life and how we need to put our time and all we are into completing the work that God has given us. Today is only a prelude to eternity and life, in one form or another, will never end for us! Thoreau caught this vision when he wrote in "Walden," "So, our human life but dies down to its root, and still puts forth its green blade to eternity."

Thoreau believed in choosing with great care what our treasure is – what is of utmost importance to us. He specifically put the following verse in the writing of "Walden" and of even more importance, our Heavenly Father sets out with great clarity these truths. Matthew 6:19-21 (NLT) "Don't store up treasures here on earth, where they can be eaten by moths and get rusty, and where thieves break in and steal. Store your treasures in heaven, where they will never become moth-eaten or rusty and where they will be safe from thieves. Wherever your treasure is, there your heart and thoughts will be also."

"Who is Somebody Else?"

"Somebody Else" is one of the most popular persons to have ever lived on this earth. This name can be used for a boy or a girl. However, for a new-born, the name does not apply. We have to be old enough to think a little bit before we can call on "Somebody Else."

In thinking back over my life, I can remember times that I would tell my Parents that this job should be turned over to "Somebody Else." I didn't see this person but he must have been there with us. Sometimes, I would be told in plain English to get up; get ready; and do the job. There was something about this "Somebody Else" that I did not like. He seemed to always be in the middle of what I ought to do when I wanted to do just what I wanted to do.

Isn't this the way all of us operate sometimes? The busier the day, the more we get pressured to take on extra chores. It surely would be comforting to have some machine that we could withdraw help from when we are over-whelmed. If banks can have ATM's why couldn't we have AFH's, Automatic Free Helps? This would be disastrous to our personalities and no one could depend on us for anything.

God does not operate His business this way. When He tells us to get up and get out and be about His business, He means for us to move. He does not entertain the notion that we could pass our work off to "Somebody Else."

A job given us by our parents; our boss where we work; or some person who has charge of us are just as valid requests as those would be directly from the Lord. God has always taught that we should honor our parents; respect our government and the officials who are over us; and most of all, that we should love Him above everything. This is life's most compelling station. If we get this part right in our lives, everything else will fall into place and we will find whatever we need to fulfill our potential. If we fail to learn how to put God first in our lives, everything will be askew and life will be tedious and unproductive.

There is a story in the Bible, Luke 10:30-37, that illustrates how we are to help persons who need us. It tells of a poor Jewish man traveling from Jerusalem on a trip to Jericho who found out about "Somebody Else" the hard way. He was beaten; stripped of his clothing and money; and left half dead beside the road. A Jewish Priest and later a man who worked in the Temple decided to pass on by and leave the man's care to "Somebody Else." Finally a despised Samaritan came along and took over the care of the injured man. He put him up on his own donkey; carried him to the nearest inn; bathed and doctored his wounds; and even left money with the innkeeper for his future care. Jesus said the Samaritan showed mercy to the injured person and that we are to go and do the same.

None of us want to be in the position of needing help. But, there may come a time in our lives that we need someone to stop; talk with us; and try to help us find a way of making it through the day. Let's hope that "Somebody Else" isn't sent to help us. When we are in dire need, our greatest desire is that God's mercy will be operating in those who are trying to care for us.

Let us hope that "Somebody Else" is kicked right out of our lives and that we will gladly try to be carriers of God's mercy to those who need us!

"God neither Slumbers nor Sleeps"

Do you have trouble sleeping when bed-time comes? Many people have this problem. There are about as many reasons for this as there are differences in each of us.

Some folks can eat a lot of spicy food, especially late in the evening, and count sheep most of the night. We can worry and try to figure out how everything is going to be and this can cause sleep to run away. Some people are in pain and cannot sleep. There are homeless people who have no bed – alone and afraid on the streets. Many things can affect our ability to sleep.

I can remember when I was little and would wake up scared after having a bad dream. Just knowing that my parents were close by would help me settle down and go back to sleep. Fear would go away because I knew they would take care of me. Perhaps this is a juvenile comparison but I believe this is the kind of trust that God wants us to place in Him.

Psalm 121:4 KJV says "Behold, he that keepeth Israel shall neither slumber nor sleep." I really wasn't sure what 'slumber' meant so I looked in the dictionary and found that 'slumber' is a light sleep – maybe like dozing. And, sleep means a giving away to rest that is deep and good.

Sleep is something we are all acquainted with and need. God made us this way. We have to rest to nourish our bodies and minds and get ready to live tomorrow. It can be a wonderful thing when we consider that God is awake and will not go to sleep. It makes it easier for us to seek sleep because we know that He is watching over us. It's hard to under- stand how God can be everywhere at the same time. His abode is in Heaven but He manages to patrol the area around our beds every night, all night long. He knows each of us and calls us by name. I think He says "don't let yourself be afraid – I am here and will take care of you."

One way to prepare for a good night's sleep is to have a productive day. When we feel that we have accomplished something of value during the day, it can help us be ready to wind down and get needed rest. And, the fact that we have had a good day today can make us feel that our next day will also be worthwhile.

As we age, we come to the place where we realize that everything does not happen in an instant. It takes time to complete anything that is valuable. When we were in school, we thought the school year would never end. Also, some of the subjects we had to learn seemed beyond our grasp. But, as the year ended, much to our surprise, we had learned the required material and were ready to pass on to the next grade. Even now as adults, we still have to learn some difficult lessons.

It takes time to build a life! Most of us know about false starts and warped commitments. I am wary of folks who try to convince us that their lives have always been full of purpose and free from friction. I've had my share of trouble, most of it brought on by my own failure to seek the "high road."

This God, who neither slumbers nor sleeps, is teaching us how to trust Him; how to trust each other; and how to trust our own judgment. At the end of the day, I love to pray this prayer – "Now I lay me down to sleep; I pray the Lord my soul to keep; if I should die before I wake, I pray the Lord my soul to take."

God's Word tells us in Psalm 4:8 (NLT) - "I will lie down in peace and sleep, for you alone, O Lord, will keep me safe."

"Let Go Of Yesterday"

Were we to be asked if we are tied to the past, most of us would emphatically deny holding on to anything that happened before today. And yet, we are all, to one degree or another, carrying around something connected to our past.

It is natural for us to remember those we love who are already gone. Part of thinking about them includes things we did together and ways they enriched our lives. Hopefully, we did the same for them. This is "good" holding on and I believe it is the stuff of which some dreams are made.

But, there is another kind of holding on that cripples our freedom and our initiative to be all that we can be. We can all remember times that we did not live up to our best. This is a very human trait. Look at the times Edison failed when he was inventing the light bulb. He did not take this as a personal affront to his intelligence but he said "this is one more way it will not work."

Down thru the years, I have read little sermons written by Dr. Norman Vincent Peale. He always encouraged "positive thinking" and his writings were filled with this theory. He wrote a wonderful book entitled "The Power of Positive Thinking" and I feel that he helped many persons change their lives for the better. He was the pastor of the great Marble Collegiate Church in New York City. How I wish I could visit this beautiful structured church where so many great giants of faith have worshiped.
Dr. Arthur Caliandro is the senior minister at this church now. He has been there since 1984 and is much loved by his congregation. His church has a program every Sunday morning at 9:30 ET on the Hallmark Channel. It is called "Simple Faith". I found it by accident several weeks ago and am thoroughly enjoying it every Sunday morning.

Dr. Caliandro is the author of several books – one being "Lost & Found." I heard him say last Sunday, "when you've done all you can do about something, let it go!" I always need to hear this said to me, and I figure some of you do, too.

Ralph Waldo Emerson voiced this same sentiment years ago. He said, "Finish each day and be done with it. You have done what you could; some blunders and absurdities have crept in; forget them as soon as you can. Tomorrow is a new day; you shall begin it serenely and with too high a spirit to be encumbered with your old nonsense."

Even farther back than this God inspired this truth in Philippians 3 vs. 13 & 14(NLT) "No, dear brothers and sisters, I am still not all I should be, but I am focusing all my energies on this one thing: Forgetting the past and looking forward to what lies ahead, I strain to reach the end of the race and receive the prize for which God, through Christ Jesus, is calling us up to heaven."

The only way we can live a life where we do not make any mistakes is to simply "do nothing." But, God makes it possible for us to correct the error of our ways – that is if we really want to. We have to be sorry before He can forgive us and we have to be sincere to want to reach for God's best. If we don't succeed at once, we keep on trying. And, God, in His own time, moves us on out a little closer to the end of the race. Perhaps, the prize for which we have been working is made up of all the dealings we have had with God and the way our faith has grown during our life-time here.

And, as Richard Bach, author said – "Here is the test to find whether your mission on Earth is finished: If you're alive, it isn't."

"God Can Make a Way When There Is No Way"

One of my Mother's favorite quotes was "there will always be a way". When I could not see a way out of something, she would tell me this. Life brings each of us to this place where our own individual crisis looms in front of us. Are we "done for" when this happens?

There are lots of "how to" books on the shelves. We are always being enticed to read and learn how to do something. But, practical books like "how to stand still and wait for God to work something out" are few and far between. There may be some on the market but most of them are hard to understand. They leave us just where they found us. . We need something that is based on the Bible, as many of them are; but we need simple language that we can understand.

This is where God's Word comes in. He can, and does, make Scriptures say what we need to know. God's Word is alive and is able to cut through all the pent-up excuses we have for not believing. And, some-times when we catch a glimpse of some particular truth in His Word, it's as though we had never read this verse before.

So, what should we do when we are so befuddled we do not know which way to turn? One thing we should not do is to "push the panic button". This is easy to do when the hurdle is very high. And, then after we push every button we know, we finally turn loose and let God have it. This is not the ideal way to deal with a problem. When time has failed to give us the answer, we should back up and put it in God's hands.

When we read Isaiah 55:8 & 9 (NLT) it helps us know that God is not surprised when we act in a manner that is childish. These verses say – "My thoughts are completely different from yours," says the Lord. "And my ways are far beyond anything you could imagine. For just as the heavens are higher than the earth, so are my ways higher than your ways and my thoughts higher than your thoughts." Ideally, we only make the mistake once of not giving God our problems but this is not true for most of us. We learn by doing something – over and over.

God is more able to make a right decision regarding our problems than anyone. Not only does He see the past roads we have traveled, He also sees the future. He knows just which way we should turn today to come out right tomorrow. There is no greater safety than being in His hands and permitting Him to guide us. And, the peace that comes when we turn our problems over to God makes us know that this is right. Sometimes, it is hard to wait for the Lord to answer but He has His time and His way of doing things and He will not be hurried.

The world's definition of happiness is linked to material things. And, we all appreciate the comforts of this day. But, just having an abundance of "things" is not the answer to real living. God made us to be dissatisfied unless we are involved in telling the world about Jesus. And, there is a private place in our hearts that only gets a work-out when we spend ourselves in the service of others. The things of God that we are learning about today will be our introduction to heaven when this life is over. Everything that we have learned, accomplished, and lived will make the journey with us into eternity. At that time, God will fashion us in His image where His thoughts and His ways will become ours – at least in part!

"I'm Always Surprised When the Cotton Opens"

I don't know what day this year I saw my first open cotton boll. This little white dot sort of peeped up above the green stalks and when I looked more closely, the open cotton was everywhere.

It is a long time from May when the cotton is planted until September or October when it is picked. It used to all be done by hand and I did my share of this, too. When I was in high school, I knew I had to work when I got home from school. In September, the sun is hot about this time in the afternoon and even the first part of October it is very warm. I can remember taking some of the money I made picking cotton and going to the local fair. I always associated this time of year with the World Series because they would announce on the loud speaker what teams were playing and what the score was.

We associate so many things with long-ago days and for me, open fields of cotton were very important. This was the best time of year to make a little extra money. The harvest, large or small, came after the rains and the sun do their job. There has to be a crop planted if we want to see live plants coming up. After that comes cultivation. The stalks mature; the blooms emerge, and then the boll opens. It is the opening of this cotton boll that always surprises me!

God's world has a certain order – to have a harvest, there must first be the planting or sowing of seed. Then, the crop must be worked, and have nourishment from the rain and sun to grow into full maturity.

You and I are sort of like this. God fashioned us before we were born. And, from the moment of birth, we are touched by our Heavenly Father and led forth into His regime of training and transformation that will help us become real children of God. We are molded, pruned, and led into ever-deepening gratitude to God whose love is so freeing and unconditional. It is so wonderful not to be condemned for anything. This is the way we are supposed to love each other because we are all in the same boat. "For all have sinned; all fall short of God's glorious standard." Romans 3:23 (NLT)

Every day brings us opportunities to observe some miracle that God provides for us. He is still in the "healing business." When our doctor needs a hand with our sickness, God is available. Medicines can be curative agents but sometimes, all that will help us is the touch of the "great Physician." Miracles happen to the young, and the old. We need to look for that "lift" that God provides for us. Only His power can make real just what we need – when we need it.

Let us look around us – the cotton is open and wonderful to see. This is a miracle we can all enjoy. May it incite us to plant seeds in our lives where the harvest will help others to see God!

"God's Rest Areas"

All of the major highways now have places to stop, areas in which we can rest. It is good to get out of the car, walk around, and let the blood circulate more freely down to our toes. These roads can take us many places and help us see many things.

I have been watching the rise and fall of the river. I heard today that the river is rising but is expected to begin a slow fall later this week. This morning I saw a piece of wood floating down-stream as usually happens when the water begins to rise. On that limb sat a bird, just riding along. I thought perhaps it was getting a drink of water and had just decided to rest before flying back toward the bank. It may have been looking for some kind of food, too. But, whatever the reason, this bird had a place of safety where it could replenish its strength and get ready for the next flight.

We are on a flight that is speeding through life, bound for our eternal home. God always gives us rest areas. Someone told me not long ago that we, God's children, get strength from each other. This is something that God can always approve. It can surely build us up when we see someone putting their all into serving the Lord. This is a sight that carries something touched with magic. And, if we can learn to be still, God will give us something that will become a part of us and better equip us for making the rest of our journey. Whatever we need is in God's store-house. He never runs out of supplies. Our journey is not similar to that of being on a run-a-way train, traveling very fast, unaided and unattended. God's schedule is always current and we will never miss our next connection. Just because we deal with health problems, family crises or other things does not mean that we are not traveling first-class. God writes our ticket but how long the journey will take is one of life's questions that remains unanswered. I am convinced that every rest area that we will need will come into sight as we go around the bend.

We will be fed as we make this trip. These bodies of ours have to be refueled and God, Who made us, is well aware of this fact. We may not eat caviar on our trip but we will have enough of what we need to live. In the story of Heidi, she and her grandfather had milk and bread as their daily food. When she left the mountain, the food set before her was quite different. But, when she returned to her grandfather and the mountain, their bread and the milk given by their goats provided just what they needed every day.

We cannot always live on the mountain-top in our walk with God. There comes a time when we have to come back down and walk our daily walk with Him. It is good to have times when we know, as the song says, that "Surely the Presence of the Lord is in This Place." As we believe, feel, and know that this Presence is with us, we can always find the rest area that we need. God understands when we have physical problems; He is concerned when we are tossed and turned with trying to decipher what His will is in a certain situation; and He is glad with our trying to learn how to "listen" to His voice. There will be days when the sun does not shine; and life becomes an up-hill journey; but, in the stillness, as we wait, we will be carried forward and we may be able to hear the "brush of angels wings."

God's thoughts are much different from ours, and His ways are so much higher than ours. We can trust Him always because of what is said in Isaiah 49:16a (Amplified Bible) - "Behold, I have indelibly imprinted (tattooed a picture of) you on the palm of each of My hands." He cannot; He will not ever forget us!

"God Offers Us Long-Term Care"

Long-term is a phrase that is relatively new. It does not mean something that is somewhat long (longish), nor does the word "long-standing" capture the real meaning even though it means something that has existed for a long time. In fact, the only use of long-term in the dictionary is in regard to long-term bonds meaning bonds that will not mature for several years or longer.

Some insurance can be bought that is classified as "long-term insurance". The first I ever heard of this was several years ago when I was being urged to buy this type of insurance. It is mainly linked to nursing home insurance and will pay for the amount of time and daily benefit that the policy provides.

Nursing home care is classified as long-term care. Some folks enter a nursing home and stay only a short time and then get able to return to their home. Others find it necessary to live there for an unlimited time. This is when long-term care is of greatest value.

When God takes us into His family, He pledges "long-term care" to us. We do not have to be concerned about His care increasing in monetary value; there are no short term pledges made to us as to our care, and there are no closing of doors prohibiting access to Him. God's workers provide everything we need and they do it with tender love and absolute caring.

God does not require that we buy long-term insurance to qualify for His family. What He does require is that we believe that He will take us in and we can enter by believing that Jesus is His Son and that He has taken care of all that needs fixing for us to be a part of this long-term family.

There is nothing more important than to know God and His plan for us to be His children. Whatever life brings through the years, and regardless of how many riches we might enjoy; if we miss cementing our relationship to God where we are bound for the promised land, we have missed it all. When life ends here, most of the things that were so important to us will be of no value then. We must learn how to live and how to pack into each day our desire to belong to God and to please Him. It has been said that the person who makes no mistakes is the one who is not doing much. God has our "back covered". When we fail, He takes up the slack and when we just half-way do something that is good, He places a "gold star" on our record.

Sometimes some people go thru the motions of being a Christian without realizing that this life we are reaching for is the only one that has real substance. Each of us must come to the place where we know that our seeking; our learning to listen to God, and our faith in Him become the long-term wind that carries us along.   And, as we live our lives, we need to each day come to a better understanding of what it means to belong to God. The Bible says in Hebrews 11:6, (NLT) - "So, you see, it is impossible to please God without faith. Anyone who wants to come to him must believe that there is a God and that he rewards those who sincerely seek him."

"May I Pay With an IOU"?

I doubt that present day businesses use a petty cash box as we used to do. Of course, our boxes did not contain great sums of money but if we needed a dollar or two, we could take the money out and put in a signed slip showing our withdrawal. There was one feature that made this pretty hectic and this was when someone forgot to put in a signed IOU.

IOU's have been around for a long time. Back in depression days, bankrupt governments used these slips of paper to pay some of their obligations. Only those creditors who were in good financial shape could afford to take these "debt slips" because sometimes they had to hold them for quite a while before someone would take them off their hands.

I'm told that our nation has a trust fund crammed with IOU's. I've read that this money has been moved out of the Social Security Fund and used for other projects. I guess this could be classified as "borrowing from Peter to pay Paul." It doesn't seem to be good fiscal responsibility for this to happen. As long as there is enough money to cover these IOU's, it isn't so terribly bad but if this were the case, there would be no need to use the "debt slips" in the first place.

There is probably not a household budget that has not had to do some wrangling from time to time. The unexpected always happens. And, when money is low, this is just the time that the car will break down; or a tooth will lose a crown; or some other every day happening will occur. This is the reason we need to put back a little money "for a rainy day." Many people today are having a hard time making ends meet. They may have had to face unemployment, sickness, or some other mountain over which they have no control.

God has a petty cash box that is filled with Heaven's treasures. We are always free to remove what we need without dropping in a "debt slip", This week I have been in great need – I misplaced my house key; I was sick in body and weary in spirit; I lost my purse with my driver's license in it, and several other things happened. Each time I went to the Lord and asked for help and He answered. He did not bring me my house key – I had to keep looking but I found it. God could have sent this key flying through the air into my hands but He does not work this way much of the time. He expects me to use up every resource I have and

48

then when I am finished, the answer comes. I might say that these seem to be ordinary circumstances, but believe me, they were quite important to me. When I was so sick, God assured me that He was with me and that He knew just what was happening. As we always say, "this, too, passed" and I was on the other side of my illness. My lost purse came about because I was not careful enough and even with this, God showed me what to do to protect myself.

I decided that it was time to pay God back for all His help. I pulled out the "debt slip" where I had asked help in finding my house key and it was neatly marked – "paid in full;" the wadded up piece of paper where I asked help when I was so sick was all smoothed out and the words written on it – "paid in full," and the slip that I had hurriedly thrown at the petty cash box asking help in finding my purse was on the very top of all the other requests stamped in red – "paid in full." I did not have to plead for help or promise that I would pay on a certain day. God just answered in His own way and in His own time.

All these things are ours because of who we are - God's children. We are immeasurably rich and I believe that God wants us to ask for whatever we need. He not only wants to give us "creature comforts," He wants us even now to begin to tap the reserves of Heaven.

One key to finding joy for our lives here and now is found in Psalm 84 vs. 10-12 (NLT)

"A single day in your courts
is better than a thousand anywhere else!
I would rather be a gatekeeper in the house of my God
than live the good life in the homes of the wicked.
For the Lord God is our light and protector.
He gives us grace and glory.
No good thing will the Lord withhold
from those who do what is right.
O Lord Almighty,
happy are those who trust in you."

"My ETA Depends on My ETD"

While I was working at Southern Towing Co., I learned some of a new language. This is nothing new – wherever we work, we soon fall into the habit of using the language of the day. A hospital emergency room is just the place to hear B/P 180/80 and perhaps instructions by the doctor in charge to send the patient to the OR. A short-order cook in a restaurant surely has a unique lingo – such as "eggs over easy," "hold the mayo," etc. Southern Towing Company's business was pushing barges loaded with grain, cement, etc. up and down several rivers and arriving at an "estimated time of arrival." This arrival date always depended on the time of departure from the loading or unloading ports.

When I begin a trip, I know that when I get there will depend a lot on when I leave. Sometimes we have delays over which we have no control and this makes our arrival late. Other times, we may stop because we choose to do so, and this can also make us late. My niece from Michigan recently came to see all of us. Her sister wanted to know what time they would arrive. She was thinking of the evening meal. They estimated that if they left at a certain time, they would be in Caruthersville in the early evening

I like to be on time when I go to Church; in fact, I like to get there a little early and then I have time to get myself settled down and get my mind quieted. To do this, my estimated time of departure must be a little after 10:00am for my estimated time of arrival to coincide with the 10:30am starting time. We miss a lot sometimes by having to hurry so much.

The length of our lives is uncertain – our estimated time of departure cannot be settled on. This has to do with God's timing. This is a timing that is fixed – not estimated. And, the time of our arrival at the gate that opens into Heaven's entities is also timing that has been fixed by God. I don't know how long it takes for us to journey from this earthly body to our heavenly home. God has this all settled and I do not have to even pack a bag.

However, this trip that we are now engaged in is called "life." There is much that we can do during our lives to ensure, not only our sure arrival up there, but also some of the so-called perks that are waiting for us.

It seems to me if I just get into the door, I will have more than I ever deserved. And, I am depending on Jesus for this. I am trying to keep things in the proper order by first of all, praying every day for God to keep things right between us. I hold on to the words found in I John 1 vs.9 (NLT) – "But if we confess our sins to him, he is faithful and just to forgive us and to cleanse us from every wrong." Sometimes, I have to ask forgiveness several times a day.

While we are here in this life, let us find our purpose for being here. This is the gateway to a wonderful life. My most precious experiences have been the times that God has made Himself known to me. He wants us to know that He approves of us and He is not stingy with His love. Whatever my estimated time of departure from this world and my estimated time of arrival in eternity are, God will work it out according to His good pleasure and this is ok with me.

"The Hiding Place"

Corrie ten Boom's life-story was told in a book and then a film entitled "The Hiding Place." She was a dedicated Christian and God used her in hiding and saving many of the Jews when Germany invaded Holland. Her life was miraculously spared when she was freed from a concentration camp. Until her death, she traveled the whole world speaking of God's love and forgiveness for each of us.

We, as mortals, are plagued with facing fear every day we live. Even the past still holds us in its grip because we cannot, or do not turn loose of the pictures in our minds that caused us the most apprehension. God wants us to trust Him to deal with our former years.

When we awake in the morning. we set in motion a chain of events that will transpire before night falls. Each hour is filled with happenings that we have begun by the actions we have taken. The other day I had a busy schedule facing me and I began the day by asking the Lord to take care of me and those whom I was helping. During the middle of the afternoon, I suffered a wreck with my car – no one was hurt but my car had to go to the hospital and my self-esteem was shaken. When someone told me that my praying had done no good, I said that had my prayer not gone up to God that morning, the other person and I might have been hurt in the wreck. We cannot see all the wheels in motion, but God is on our side every moment of every day!

Once in awhile, I try to out-guess God as to my future. Questions come, one after another – what is going to happen to me; will I be able to take care of, not only myself but others who are my responsibility; how can I enlarge their lives – not only with the necessities, but with sharing eternal truths? If I help to provide food, clothing, and shelter for them and do not convince them that God loves them, I have failed in making concrete their eternal future.

Life here is hard sometimes and we very much need to know with our minds that God is real. Help and comfort are available to us every day. We never out-grow needing that unexpected lift that happens when God comes to our aid. His help is invaluable but there is almost something magical that happens within our hearts. As we begin to realize that God is with us, the physical help we needed becomes almost obscure and we just want to concentrate on His nearness!

Perhaps we spend our whole lives learning how to face death. Just knowing that death is inevitable doesn't make us capable of facing it. As we grow older, hopefully we can look back and see that the "hand of God" has been our "guiding light". Nothing we have faced; nothing we have endured has been wasted. All the happenings, knowledge, impressions that we have experienced are now a part of who we are. And every day we keep on trying to learn how to live, and also how to die. Death is a natural part of life and something each of us must face. But we can trust God to take care of every detail of this and every experience.

When Corrie ten Boom was a little girl in Holland, she tells of being with her father and talking about her fear of dying. She said, "Papa, what is it like to die"? Father ten Boom replied, "When you and I go to Amsterdam, when do I give you your ticket"? Corrie answered, "Just before we get on the train". Her father told her, "So it is with death. When the time comes, you will look into your heart and find the strength you need – just in time."

"Thou art my hiding place and my shield; I hope in thy word." Psalm 119:114

"We Spend Our Lives as a Tale That Is Told"

Psalm 90 is a narrative that describes our lives while we are here and even before we were born into this world. It begins by asserting that God has been the dwelling place of all generations. It alludes to the age old question – how long has God existed. And, it declares that God has been – from everlasting to everlasting!

A thousand years in God's sight are but as yesterday when it is past and the "hustle and bustle" of our lives is spent as a "tale that is told." Whether the days of our years are threescore years and ten, or they are fourscore years, they are over too quickly. For our time comes and we fly away! The secret of living a great life is to follow the Lord and invest all that we are in fulfilling His plan for us. God wants us to be happy every day that we live. Some days will undoubtedly bring problems and trouble that we have to deal with but even when our emotions are in upheaval, we can still have the deep, abiding love with which God showers us. No two of us express our emotions in exactly the same way and this is good. I find myself crying, whether I am sad or happy. You might not shed a tear but your way is right for you and my way is right for me.

I believe that God receives the love that we send to Him and that He understands "why we cry or why we do not." But, there is a layer of knowledge deep within the soul that worships God in a very unique way. It is sort of like "a well of living water" that is pushing truth upward into our reach. It seems to me that all we need do to experience this deep, deep knowledge is to just let ourselves be aware of God's inner-working within us. He always knows how to communicate with us.

God wants our lives to be useful to Him. He gives each of us talents to use in showing others that He loves them, too. Some folks believe that being called into the ministry or any church-related vocation is really a calling to "full time Christian service." And, I believe this, too. However, I also believe that each of us has been called into "full time Christian service." God wants each of us for His use, and He wants us to serve Him every day of our lives.

God's beauty will "rub off" on what we do, and who we are, if we will permit Him to use us in carrying out His plan for all the people of the

53

world. Everyone needs to know God, Jesus Christ, and the Holy Spirit! We don't have to understand all that makes God Who He is. Most of us would certainly fall short if this were one of the requirements for God using our lives. This does not give us leeway to wallow in ignorance – we are to study God's Word and to earnestly try to be the best person that we can be.

May every year that we are permitted to live enrich the story of our lives. May we spend our years as a tale that is told! And, may the beauty of the Lord make us what He wants us to be!

"What Will Stand The Test Of Time?"

Ford Motor Company is over 100 years old now. Henry Ford and his Model T etched their place in the progress of our country. Mr. Ford used to say, "You can have any color you want so long as it's black." He wanted every person to be able to own an automobile and this is almost true in our country today. One hundred years seems to be what we consider "old", whether it applies to a company, an antique, or a person.

The criteria for whether or not a piece of furniture can be classified as an antique used to be its age and 100 years was the acceptable definition. Today, in addition to the 100 year age factor, other things figure into whether or not a chair or table are antiques such as the period that defines this particular piece of furniture.

I think it is quite astonishing when a person lives to be 100 years old. They have seen the beginning and ending of many days. At one time, their lives were full and productive. But, the time for work has its limits and age carries the chair of inactivity. So many people in facilities for the aged and handicapped live entirely different from the way they used to live. And, one thing they have in common is the desire to "go home." What a blessing our home is and how it comforts us during good times and bad.

Time changes everything. Ford Motor Company is not what it was 100 years ago and I imagine Mr. Ford would be so proud if he could see their cars today. This is a work of progress and the bustling day's work is to produce more and better cars at a price the average person can afford. Antique lovers weigh the advantages that the years bring to their trade. And, we, of human frame, marvel at the passing years and praise God for allowing us to stay here and participate in life as we know it.

Day by day, we are constantly changing – hopefully for the better. It behooves us to use our time wisely, giving first place to what is important to us in our lives. No one can fill our niche. To fail in finding God's plan for our lives is to short-change not only our joy here but whatever kind of reward system God has planned for all of us when this life is over.

The only things that will stand the test of time are those connected to God's highest purposes. Simplicity may be one of the keys for finding and experiencing God's best.
It's the little things that make for real living. A word spoken at the right time can be the way out for someone; a smile can be just as real as a cup of cold water; and the clasp of a hand can help us recharge our batteries and get back out into the race of life.

Many voices clamor for our attention. We already have what we need to live a good life here. God took care of all of this when the Holy Spirit came to indwell us. All we have to do is to try and live out what we know inside. These are the things that will stand the test of time. Henry Wadsworth Longfellow surely caught the vision when he wrote –

"A Psalm of Life"

Tell me not, in mournful numbers,
Life is but an empty dream!-
For the soul is dead that slumbers,
And things are not what they seem.

Life is real! Life is earnest!
And the grave is not its goal;
Dust thou art, to dust returnest,
Was not spoken of the soul.

Lives of great men all remind us
We can make our lives sublime,
And, departing, leave behind us
Footprints on the sands of time;

Footprints, that perhaps another,
Sailing o'er life's solemn main,
A forlorn and shipwrecked brother,
Seeing, shall take heart again.

Let us, then, be up and doing,
With a heart for any fate;
Still achieving, still pursuing,
Learn to labor and to wait."

"We Are All Athletes in God's Sight"

Thousands of people converged on Athens, Greece in 2004 to celebrate the Summer Olympics. Some were athletes; others were spectators. It was a very large gathering with people coming from practically every country in the world.

Opening night saw the athletes march in under the cover of their national flag. Some participants were well known; others were hoping they would win Olympic medals. In this setting, competition is keen and to win a gold medal is the highest prize there is.

This made me think of another day that is coming for all of us. When life, as we know it, is over and God's time has come for "the judging," there will be a gathering of people so large that it will make the attendance at the Olympics look small in comparison. Every person who has ever lived will be there. Revelations 20 vs. 12 & 13 (The Living Bible) tells about this coming event. – "I saw the dead, great and small, standing before God; and The Books were opened, including the Book of Life. And the dead were judged according to the deeds he had done. The oceans surrendered the bodies buried in them; and the earth and the underworld gave up the dead in them. Each was judged according to his deeds."

Television advertised the Olympics for a long time before the games began. God's plan is so much better – His Word has been sent out for centuries warning all of us about this day that is coming and stating that each of us will participate. We have been admonished that this very important day will prove whether or not God has accepted our deeds.

God does everything in order – His order – and to make our lives count for good, we must initially become connected to Him. He initiates the search for us and when we pledge our allegiance to Him, our lives change direction. He cleans us up; opens the "prayer-waves" between us and Heaven, and shows us how to follow Him. This is not a lesson that we learn in one sitting; it takes a lifetime to make us ready to appear before God in that day when the Book of Life will be opened.

God wants us to learn to be sensitive to His voice, and to the way He leads us. We are His sheep and we are to learn the sound of His voice. He knows all about us – nothing surprises Him that we do – or do not do. I am convinced that God can take any life and make it equal to any performance from an Olympic athlete.

This day will differ from the Olympics in this way - in the games each athlete wants to win the gold to further his or her career. In the events of God's "judging", our motive will be to love God and to please Him. On that day, pleasing our Heavenly Father will be its own reward. And, until that time comes, we live our lives on a daily basis, training as good soldiers of Jesus Christ. We learn that there is no higher motive in living than to be a part of God's work in saving the world.

Because we have thrown our lot in with God, we live each day with its wins and defeats. Just because we lose a battle does not mean that we have lost the war. God is always cheering us on from the sidelines but this is not all – when we belong to Him, He actually lives within us providing the steam we need for each moment of the day. And, when our lives are tallied up, we can face the results without fear because God, who has been our companion for such a long time, will still be everything we need on that day!

"I'm Grateful for Everything"

My Niece, Linda Cowen, lives at the Caruthersville Nursing Center, Caruthersville, Mo. Every time I am involved with any of the people over there, whether they are residents or staff, I come away with a new sense of the wonder of God's love. We are all so different – male and female; white and black; old in years and not so old; and, different disabilities that make it necessary for us to be there.

Some of the people there, like my niece, have to be fed; some find it hard to swallow; and all are living in their own worlds. But, the same could be said for those of us who are guests – we all occupy our own worlds and are so fortunate when we can let others in to communicate with us. Shelia Brown is the administrator at the Nursing Center and is so caring. She seems to know just what to do for everyone.

Even those who are not so alert have their moments when something seems to reach them, wherever they are. And, these people who work with our loved ones, day in and day out, know that they are making a difference in people's lives. My niece tells them how much she loves them and she knows most of them by name. I know from helping my Mother the last ten years of her life how hard it is to see our folks old and sick. And, my heart fills up with pride in the human race when I see how folks who live there are treated with such compassion and understanding.

This might be a little odd for a tribute to Thanksgiving but, to me it is fitting. We love our people, regardless of what kind of shape they are in and we feel gratitude to those who care for them. None of us know what the future holds for us. This is not morbid thinking – it is just being realistic and making peace within ourselves as to how to look at the upcoming days.

I now know, as I did not know before my niece went into the nursing center that we must think of the future as our friend and ally. Nothing can happen to us where God cannot get to us. When we get physically incapacitated, there is always help of some kind available to us. When life has dealt us a blow and we are "down and out", there is always someone or something that picks us up. And, when our consciousness is dimmed, I believe that God is right where we are and that He never leaves us.

I am thankful for all that God sends to make us happy people. And, I am also thankful for the somber side of life that each of us will one day walk through. I believe what I am learning is that wherever we are bedded down for today is right where God can see us. As long as we can reach out and touch Him, we don't have to be afraid of anything!

Hopefully each Thanksgiving that comes around will bring us closer to God where we can feel and know that He has charge of us and that whatever comes, does so with His permission. We need to learn how to be thankful in our hearts. Maybe we can figure out how to let go of age old questions like "how and why certain things happened or did not happen." The most important thing is – that we be grateful to God for all He has done for us down through the years. Every breath we take is a gift from God. Wherever we live; whatever our condition; we are important to someone. And, we are all important to God!

"For in him we live and move and are! As one of your own poets says it, 'We are the sons of God.' Acts 17 v 28 (The Living Bible).

"Knowing God Is Our Greatest Privilege"

Psalm 42 vs. 1 tells of the correlation between a deer's thirst for water and our hunger and thirst to know God.

The Living Bible reads – "As the Deer pants for water, so I long for you, O God."

The New International Reader's Version says – "A deer longs for streams of water. God, I long for you in the same way."

The Contemporary English Version says – "As a deer gets thirsty for streams of water, I truly am thirsty for you, my God."

The New American Standard Bible says – "As the deer pants for the water brooks, So my soul pants for You, O God."

The Message reads – "A white-tailed deer drinks from the creek; I want to drink God, deep draughts of God."

Regardless of how we say it, every version mentioned above speaks of our need to know God. This is not something that only I need, it is a common meeting place for every human soul. God made us to be a part of Him and this can come thru longing, thirsting, panting, and drinking. Our seeking to find and make God a part of our lives was not meant to be so complicated that we would get lost in the shuffle and quit trying. It only gets hard to understand when what He says does not go along with what we want to believe and do. We have the option of choosing what we believe and how we want to live our lives.

We need to be so glad when we find ourselves longing to know God. We have been brought to this place through God's intervention in our lives. Only He has the power to make us realize how empty we are without Him. He places love so deep in us that we want to give it back to Him.

God's Word becomes new to us. We are now able to be still for a few minutes and read our Bibles. And, wonder of wonders, we begin to understand just a little of what it says. We read about our Heavenly Father, Who created the world and us; about Jesus, Who died for our sins; and about this wonderful person of the Holy Spirit, Who is along-side us every minute of every day. Our thirst grows to know more and more about this God – Who is three persons in one. This thirsting is our ally – something that keeps us on the move to explore and accept new dimensions of our universe and our place in it.

When a deer pants for water, he is very thirsty. It is a matter of "life and death." He might be able to go for awhile without this water, but eventually his system would shut down and he would die. The same is true for us – when God brings us to the place where we are panting to know Him in new ways; where we have been led to see that this is the real goal of our lives; then we are in the proper position to have His blessing. We know that not following our quest will be the death of us. Physical death is not all life is about – there are eternal things to think about. But, even now when we are still here in this world, panting for God is a prelude to the opening of doors that we never knew existed.

So, we use our heads and our hearts and we DRINK. This water that comes from God is filled with all kinds of life-giving ingredients. It is sort of like baking-soda. It can bubble over very easily and we can find ourselves experiencing the magic of God's over-flowing joy. I used to tell my Mother not to cry so easily and now I find myself crying at everything – not only sad things but also when I am happy. I don't want to ever be ashamed of expressing my feelings – whether I am understood or not. I believe that being able to feel emotion, as well as to know God's Truth, are two of His gifts to us.

May we, as long as we live, long to know more about God; thirst for His fellowship; pant for the living water; and be able to drink from whatever cup He places before us. Since God instigated this search within us, He will never disappoint us.

"How to Live a 'Let-Go' Life"

I have seen times that I have been so tied-up, I could not function very well. All of us have periods of inactivity where our daily schedules are interrupted. Some of us may have times when we cannot eat, or sleep and we are anxious about many things. This is not a good way to live and one with which the Lord does not want us to socialize. Life has a way of bringing trauma to all of us and until we find the point of release in our minds, we stay this way.

I am convinced that God is always working to liberate us – from whatever has us hog-tied. The mind, heart and emotions are woven together and when one part is crippled, the whole is hampered. God frees us, moment by moment, by changing the way we think. Romans 12:2 explains that God makes us into new persons by helping us think in new ways and He helps us see that we will always have a place in God's order of things. Some market jobs require that an employee have a probationary period of learning and if they progress ok, they become permanent employees. God does not work this way. There is no period of time setting up a standard of accomplishment by a certain date. God takes us just as we are and begins a rigorous teaching program that will extend to the end of our lives. He never charts us in a negative way, and He is always sending out new ideas to help us see things in a different way.

We sometimes think of God as a reigning Monarch in heaven who is trying to make us into folks who live wonderful lives; the idea being that He cannot love us unless we are perfect in the way we think, act, and live our lives. If this were true, no one would ever come into the intimacy of being God's child because we are all imperfect. When we can see that God loves us "in spite of", we can begin to turn loose of ourselves, and learn to relax knowing that God will never "let go of us."

The art of "letting go and letting God" is one that is accessible to each of us. I didn't used to know that God is more interested in helping me than I am in asking for His help. There is talk today in the field of geriatrics that says in the years to come that aged people will live one hundred years, and some people, even longer. In all probability, if I were still alive then, I would want to live to these new projections.

But, today, we are here and life is what it is. I believe there are new ideas; pieces of knowledge; and particles of common sense called "truth" that we have never experienced. Perhaps the real goal of our lives should be in maturing to the point where we can "hang loose" so that we can absorb whatever God is sending our way.

I know that the "let-go-life" is possible, profitable, and even necessary if we are to be the persons God envisions us to be! The "how to" do this is found in Romans 12:2, (NLT) when we are told to "let God transform us into new persons by changing the way we think."

"What Makes Life Precious To You"

Thanksgiving is over; relatives have gone home; and the left-overs have all been eaten.

We're back to the same old routine – jobs and school. Some folks think when you are retired, you don't have anything special to do. Others believe that taking care of a family is just "old-hat." But, I know that life always hold a challenge whatever we use to fill our days.

No activity is "hum-drum" as long as we are consciously trying to follow the Lord. I realize sometimes that our accomplishments might look very small but if we had an instrument that could calibrate everything in our past with God's plan for us today, we might be seen in a different light. You see, I don't know what your hurts did to you or how life's entire trauma affected your life. We are all products of everything that has touched us.

I have made peace with the mistakes of my past. I do not glorify them but I accept what they did to me as just this – my past - that has been forgiven and forgotten by my Heavenly Father. Each of us is responsible for ourselves – others may be involved but in the final analysis, we made the choices that make us what we are today.

For me, life is great because I am learning that the relationship between God and His children is real. I don't hear a human voice but God speaks to me inside. Sometimes, I read some verse in the Bible and for some unknown reason, I can understand what it means. He has many ways of directing our paths and there are times I know that a certain action is the way for me to go. Other times, I may be perplexed and not know what to do or what to say, especially when I am trying to comfort someone. But, I believe that the spoken word is often forgotten but the love that prompts us to help someone is remembered and does bring comfort. Love, that puts out a hand to someone in need, makes its way into the heart and life of a person and this has to be the work of God because we have no power to ignite the heart of another!

So, we take into account our immediate past. We settle differences, if any exist, between ourselves and God; between ourselves and others; we hold up our heads, and let the sunshine of all that God is touch us. I have my moments of doubt, fear, loneliness, and   confusion. But, God always comes through and He knows just how to scatter the dark and help me see that I am not alone!

 The thing I value most about life is knowing that God lives in my heart and that He has chosen to use me to write for Him. I may not always have the language in exactly the proper form, but I know that God is try-ing to say something to me and to those who read these words. We don't have to learn a foreign language to communicate with Him. If we cannot understand what He is saying, it is not His fault – it is always ours.

Whatever makes us "tick" is part of what makes us who we are. Love is the key – and God honors us by making life priceless!

"We can rejoice, too, when we run into problems and trials for we know that they are good for us – they help us learn to be patient. And patience develops strength of character in us and helps us trust God more each time we use it until finally our hope and faith are strong and steady. Then, when that happens, we are able to hold our heads high no matter what happens and know that all is well, for we know how dearly God loves us, and we feel this warm love everywhere within us because God has given us the Holy Spirit to fill our hearts with his love." Romans 5:3-5, (The Living Bible)

"God's Family Tree"

Only recently have I become interested in the information that is shown on a family tree. It takes a lot of work to find all these facts, compile them in the proper order, and then make them a part of the family tree.

Our ancestors were real people who lived their lives in a world entirely different from ours today. But, they had their dreams, goals, and areas of accomplishment. Some are remembered for their notoriety; others bore the stigma of being victims of some evil done to them, and still a few are remembered for something good they did that has lasted down thru the years.

What will our family tree show for us? Will we be remembered just as an after-thought or will we be an important part of our ancestry? Making a name for ourselves is nothing if this is our motive for doing so. Being used of God to carry out some delegated task is enough motive in itself to carry us thru a lifetime.

History bears record of past events, purposes of actions, and results of the acts whether good or bad. We would probably be surprised if we knew everything about our ancestors. They were people just like us, made up of a mixture of good and bad. Many things in life are hidden from us as to what makes us tick; why we do things as we do; and even how we deal with our problems.

What we are gets across to people by the way we act. What we want to become might not be as obvious. This is the real walk-way between God and us – where He communes with us and changes us. There is a link between our heads and our hearts and God needs to have the key to get into both areas. It is not the big stuff that makes us what we want to be but the little things that come to us and make us quiet, gentle, and loving. Our Pastor's childrens' sermons are for "little ears" but I find myself involved, soaking it all in, and emitting, (I hope), some of the joy I am feeling. It is good to identify with something that we can understand and incorporate into our lives.

Jesus' ancestry is told in the Bible where we can see the human profile completely submerged by the divine. Our position on God's family tree shows the human part of us, also. This is the element that gains us entry to God's Family Tree. We are human now but we have the divine living inside our hearts. We are a part of God's family tree and this means our future is all wrapped up in Him. We cannot go wrong because He has charge of our past, our present, and our future! This is God's gift to us and it will never be outdated. To belong to God and He to us is what makes every day we live so beautiful!

> "God is great; God is good, let us thank Him for our food –
> and for everything that makes our lives so full."

"Does God Really Care"

Trouble has hounded me for several days and naturally I have been praying to God about my problems. I have not heard any supernatural sounds such as the ringing of bells or the blast of trumpets, and have not felt the air moving around me as from unseen angel wings. My home shows no sign of heavenly occupancy. My bed is empty except for Gracie Le, my youngest cat, and my computer has not come through with singing messages of hope and good cheer. Does this mean God has not heard my cries for help and that in spite of His saying that He would never leave me, has He departed my life?

NO – when all our clamor is over, and our strivings for His attention are finished, He comes into our consciousness and permits us to know that He is aware of everything that is going on with us and that He has it all "under control." We are just not smart enough to understand how He works. Perhaps if we could, our trust in Him would be more complete. His ways are past finding out but His interest in us never dies!

As we go through life, many hurts and obstacles hit us. But, this is not to be the focus of our lives. We are to show that we are more than conquerors through Christ. Many backward glances momentarily frighten us and we wonder how in the world we came through those years with their trauma. And then, this sweet stillness creeps into our emotions and dominates the deepest part of our hearts and we know that this whole business of God and His caring for us is real. It is a very sober-ing thing when we realize for sure that Christ lives in us and that He will never, under any circumstance, leave us.

"And I am convinced that nothing can ever separate us from his love. Death can't, and life can't. The angels can't, and the demons can't. Our fears for today, our worries about tomorrow, and even the powers of hell can't keep God's love away. Whether we are high above the sky or in the deepest ocean, nothing in all creation will ever be able to separate us from the love of God that is revealed in Christ Jesus our Lord!"

Once we realize that God cannot and will not ever leave us, we can begin to believe Romans 8 v 28,(NLT) – "And we know that God causes everything to work together for the good of those who love God and are called accord-ing to his purpose for them." God really cares for us and He always will!

"Valentine's Day Is So Much Fun!"

Valentine's Day always comes on February 14th. It has gotten to be a very big holiday. Many valentines are mailed and the post office depart-ment would tell us that this day's mail is second in size to Christmas.

I wonder what it is that makes this day so special. Perhaps, it is because it is a fun day with us being so ready to tell others how much we love them. It is not a day for doing practical jokes on someone, but essentially it is a day we can express appreciation, recognition, and high favor to whomever we wish without being thought of as "old-fashioned or pecu-liar."

It is true that anytime we tell someone how much we love them, whatev-er method we use, we get the feeling that this was a good thing to do. When I was in grade-school, we even dared to give someone a valentine without their knowing that we had a secret crush on them. It is good to tell our families that we love them – I always had something for my

Mother on special days. And, it made her happy to be remembered. Every day of our lives should be filled with attention to God's Presence with us and to the direction He is pointing out for us. We also must take care of our obligations – our families; our jobs; and our financial responsibilities. There is still enough time left during each 24 hr. period for good, clean fun. We might not like doing the same things but there is enough variety in the world for each of us to claim what we consider fun.

Whenever I take my car to be serviced, they drain out the old oil and replenish with new oil that is full of just the right ingredients for my car's motor. This must be done every 3,000 miles to keep a car in good running condition. God made us to need different things to have abundant life and one of them is to be able to care for people and to have them care for us. And, inter-mingled with this is the shared ability to have real fun just being together. Simply being with them holds the key to real fun.

It is so good to laugh – and so relaxing. Seeing and hearing some folks laugh makes us want to know what is going on. Life doesn't have to be so serious that it swallows up having a good time. Not just laughing – but even sharing a smile with someone is great!

So, let's make ourselves "fun" for someone this Valentine's Day. God will approve because He understands our need for social belonging. And, even more than this, God tells us in I John 4 v 7 (KJV) – "Beloved, let us love one another: for love is of God; and everyone that loveth is born of God, and knoweth God."

The Testing of a Proverb

"IF MARCH COMES IN LIKE A LION, WILL IT GO OUT LIKE A LAMB?"

I used to hear my Mother say every year, "it looks like March is coming in like a lion and you know if it comes in like a lion, it will go out like a lamb." Older people used to really believe in these sayings. I have even found myself quoting her by saying, "Well, March came in like a lion, so, it has to go out like a lamb."

The only way we can test these sayings, or proverbs, is to actually look and see if they do what they say. Proverbs in the Bible is a collection of sayings written before Christ came. The book of Proverbs was written by Solomon, the wisest man who ever lived. But, it is not just a collection of sayings like the old-timers remembered; it contains many short, simple statements about how to live wisely.

Proverbs 9:10 says, "Fear of the Lord is the beginning of wisdom." Respect for God was the foundation of these wise sayings. Probably the verse most familiar to most of us from the Book of Proverbs is "Trust in the Lord with all your heart; do not depend on your own understanding. Seek his will in all you do, and he will direct your paths." Proverbs 3:5 (NLT)

To see if this verse works – try it! When we find ourselves in a quandary and momentarily lost, these are the words we need to hear. And, when God gives us a push, we can decide to try it and see - "not if it works" but "how it works."

So many things happen that we cannot understand – maybe we have to get older to be able to try another way of looking at our problems. In learning the computer, I have found that there are several ways of doing something. The results may be the same but how we got there can vary. I believe God has many plans for our lives. I've heard it said "to miss one calling is to fill our lives with failure." I now know that God has alternate plans for our fulfillment. Who is to say what was the original and best plan for our lives? God knows the desire of our hearts and has promised to give us fullness of life. He is not hampered by time – we come to know that we are neither too old nor too unimportant to have God make His abode in our hearts. We learn that life is really a day by day trust. We would not be here today if it did not please God for this to be so.

I don't believe that God is standing by with a paddle to punish us for our failure to live up to His expectations. Rather, He has fashioned a large, yellow star to pin to our record just as soon as we turn to Him for forgiveness and a new start.

How March comes in is the Lord's work – whether it is like a lion or a lamb. His plan still exists for the world – and for you and me. When the winds of March are blowing, it may be that God is cleaning up the debris left from winter's blast of cold air. Is this so different from what He does in our hearts – by sweeping out the residue of sin and filling the spaces with peace and purpose?

When the breezes of March are gentle, like a lamb, the wind chimes make their soft music. And, when we get still enough, we can know that life's most precious gift is knowing that God really lives in our hearts and that He wants to have fellowship with us day by day, moment by moment.

"Look For A Surprise Today"

Hardly a day goes by that something doesn't happen that surprises us. And, I am talking about good surprises. Our main problem is that we quit looking for something to brighten our day and we miss some of life's sweetest blessings.

When I was growing up, we lived in the country and we would come to town on Saturday night, park on Ward Avenue and watch the people go up and down the street. If you've never done this, you have missed a lot. There is nothing more interesting or surprising than the things that people do and say. We, who did this, all shared a common kind of life – our entertainment was sparse and we had to find ways to have fun. It was nice and surprising to see someone we liked walking toward us. And, we always were interested in what was happening to them and surprised when they recounted something good that had happened or was coming up. To share in someone else's good fortune is a second-hand blessing – but it is a blessing never-the-less.

We don't have to look for the hard things of life – they come to everybody, in one way or another. But, the folly of it is, that when we concentrate on harboring the negative things that come, we don't have room or time in our lives to look for the surprises of today. It has been said that "life is a lot what we make it." Some things are beyond our control but our attitudes, our trust in God and our love of life will see us through many hardships.

Back in the 1920's, a new show came out called "Sally." The music for this show was written by Jerome Kern and the title song was "Look for the Silver Lining." I have always heard of "the silver lining" but I did not know it was from a musical until I researched it. Here is the way it goes:

"Look for the silver lining
When e'er a cloud appears in the blue,
Remember some where the sun is shining,
And so the right thing to do,
Is make it shine for you.

A heart, full of joy and gladness,
Will always banish sadness and strife.
So always look for the silver lining,
And try to find the sunny side of life."

In the time between Thanksgiving and Christmas, there is always a lot to do. In this in-between time, maybe we can adjust our priorities and "look for the silver lining." This morning when I got up, it was cloudy and cold. About noon, the sun burst through and it made all the difference in how the day looked and felt. Keeping my life moving on an even keel is my responsibility. It is easy to get depressed and want to quit trying. But, God is our helper and we may feel down but we don't have to stay down. God says in I Thessalonians 5:18, (KJV) – "In everything give thanks: for this is the will of God in Christ Jesus concerning you." Since this is the way we are to live, we can walk "On the Sunny Side of the Street."

"Grab your coat and take your hat
Leave your worries on the doorstep
Life can be so sweet
On the sunny side of the street."

"The Lion and the Lamb – Fact or Fiction"

As February edges out on 28 or 29 days, March comes on the horizon. Will it come in like a "lion or a lamb?" And, is the theory right that says it will go out the opposite way it enters? Who set up this idea anyway? I don't know where all the "sayings" came from but most of the generation that my Mother fit into pretended to believe these quaint theories.

Life is a lot like this – sometimes we pretend to believe in something, without actually knowing much about the subject – it tends to make us feel good and knowledgeable. Today it is popular to say we are Christians, that is if we do not have to go through too much of a change in our way of life. But, the sad part of this is that God sees what is on the inside of us and He knows if we are just "marking time" to help folks see us in a good light. I do not think every Christian is like this but I know that we want others to think well of us. I think that God made us this way. But, it can be quite tempting to try to paint ourselves in a good light, whether or not we fit into this "walk that is on the high road."

All of this was said to enforce the thought that day by day our lives amount to much more than we will ever realize. Every gesture that we make; every smile that we put out; every prayer that we say for someone; every iota of love that we project to anyone makes our lives full of the most powerful thing in the world. Sometimes, our love for someone may be shown with spontaneous fervor – like the force of the lion pictured in the month of March. Other times, we may experience a deep, quiet, beautiful warmth that exhibits the quietness of the lamb. The closest we may ever be to Heaven while we are here in this world may be the times that we feel the love of God flowing thru us, making contact with another human being.

We know it is the real thing because we are caught up in something that is bigger than ourselves. And, what a joy to have this leavening substance dwelling in us where we are cut down to size, but at the same time, we are made to be God's helpers. Real living commences when we quit pretending to be anything other than what we are - just ordinary children of God. There is no need to try to manipulate people because we learn that God can and will supply whatever we need. The most wonderful thing about this for me is to know that He really and truly knows what I need and that He has the power to move someone toward me who can help me.

Today I was very humbled when four people went out of their way to do something for me. I jokingly said, "I hope I am not getting set up to leave this world right now." When we are well and can do things for ourselves, we do not think about others coming to our rescue. But, as we get older and sometimes need help, it is so comforting to know that God has His way of taking care of us.

My wind chimes are already 'singing'. It is their introduction to the coming of March whether the air is blowing with great force or whether the gentle breezes tell us that spring is near. I used to not know that God is so real and so caring but He is helping me see that everyday is His opportunity to lead, protect and use me. These out-stretched hands and hearts that made me so happy today show how God takes care of our needs. And, whether March first is a blustery day or a day of gentle wind, the lion and the lamb each belong to God - as do we. We need not be afraid anymore because God says in Psalm 23 v 6, (KJV). "Surely goodness and mercy shall follow me all the days of my life: and I will dwell in the house of the Lord for ever!"

"What Happens To All Our Prayers?"

I sometimes wonder what kind of filing system God uses to keep track of our prayers. We pray many times during a 24 hr. period. Perhaps our prayers that need a quick answer are taken care of shortly after we seek God. Maybe they are then filed away in a finished file.

But, what about the prayers that we pray and God doesn't answer right away? Sometimes, God lets us know in a short time that our request is not in His plan. I guess we have all come to the place where we realized that we were asking for something that was not good for anyone.

And, then when God rejected our plea, we already knew that we were not praying with very much intelligence.

God has to deny our requests many times – for many reasons. We don't always know just how we are to pray and for what we are to ask. Some folks believe that to get our prayers answered swiftly and completely, we must bombard God's switchboard. They think we must demand the answer we want and even glibly quote God's Word to Him. To me this is not the way. We can come to God for help, knowing that He is willing to help us, without asserting any kind of demanding status. Who are we that we demand anything from the God of the universe? As long as we seek Him with a humble spirit, and are willing to accept His answer, He is pleased to hear us!

There is no telling how many prayers we have sent up to God during our lives. Many have been answered; some denied because they were not best for us and others; and some are still pending waiting for God's attention. He is constantly changing us into His likeness and some of this metamorphosis comes about because of our prayers. We know that God directs our prayer life – we would not know even the tiniest thing about this kind of living if He did not teach us.

Some of our daily discomfort comes because God is 'making us over'. All of our heart-felt joy is his daily gift to us. Prayer isn't just uttered and we 'trash it'. God takes seriously what we pray for and He takes us at our word and begins to answer our request in a manner that is pleasing to Him. Praying is serious business – one that carries eternal consequences.

I still do not completely understand what happens when we pray for someone. I know that God is already aware of this person's need and that He is already actively working out His 'growing' plan. But, I know from experience that when someone prays for us, it makes life easier and helps us keep the proper perspective on whatever our problem is. God doesn't always take away our problem – but He always stays with us and helps us cope daily.

These words that we speak: in prayer; to: Our Heavenly Father; are: cleaned with God's filter and made acceptable to Him. He knows how to not only clean up our hearts and our lives but also our language.

We have a lot going for us – all the prayers that we have prayed during the past years of our lives, are still alive and getting God's attention. Prayers for health have been heard and put in God's daily view; prayers for the safety of our loved ones are still in God's open file; and prayers for our spiritual maturity are helping us in our longing to truly belong to God and please Him in all that we do.

To pray is normal; to believe is life-changing; and to trust God is the secret to life!

Psalm 61 v 1 (NLT) – "O God, listen to my cry! Hear my prayer!

"We May Be Down, But We're Not Out"

All life is a struggle! God made it this way. We can have days of absolute happiness and then we can be brought up short when something happens that is out of the ordinary. From the very start of our existence, we move around in our Mother's womb throwing up our arms, kicking with our legs and feet, and moving our head. I'm told this exercise is crucial for an unborn child and it helps the Mother, also. God's best plan for our lives starts with our being motivated by Him to participate in life in this small way. With every beat of our heart, we assert our willingness to be born and to learn to live in this new environment. We come into this world with a loud cry. We assert our birthright. This is our place that God has picked out for us and though we may not know who He is at the time, this is the beginning of His purpose for our being here. God wants us to be proud (yet humble); He wants us to self-confident (yet consenting to His being the Lord of our lives); and He desires that we find the secret of life (by discovering that only living in His Presence brings real joy).

As the years pass, we begin to understand that were our lives to never "hit a snag" or if nothing happened to disrupt our feeling of peace and contentment, we would be almost like robots. It is a fact that character only develops under pressure. God has told us that He holds our hand and we cannot completely fall. But, when we are reeling from some blow to the head; some wound to the heart; and something that threatens to "get us" – let us remember that in boxing lingo, we may be down, but we are not out!

One of these days, every knee shall bow in God's Presence and the day of great discovery for us is when we learn that this is the proper stance for us right now while we are traveling through this world. I don't believe that God is primarily interested in whether or not we are actually on our knees, but He does want "our hearts to kneel." Whether we are physically walking; verbally talking; or mentally thinking; we can keep our connection to God in good repair and take Him with us into every avenue of our lives.

We are short-changing ourselves if we have not discovered that life is more than "doom and gloom." God wants us to learn to get up in the morning expecting the day before us to be full of "candy" blessings. If we are diabetic, God will even feed us with "sugar-free" sweets. The day may bring thunder, lightening, and rain storms, but every day has to have a mixture of pleasure and distress. And, whether there is more grief than joy on this day, we learn that there will never be another day just like today and tomorrow will be sent to us with God's own ingredients. Nothing can be repeated – each day has its own reward.

Life is so challenging – and I believe God wants to show us something beautiful every day. We were made to enjoy life and not to be dismayed when we get hit and momentarily lose our balance. Let us remember – we may be down – but we're not out!

We are in training to be good soldiers for God and we have the proper banner going before us which says –"Surely goodness and mercy shall follow me all the days of my life: and I will dwell in the house of the Lord for ever." Psalm 23 v. 6, (KJV)

"Jesus Is the Wind Beneath Our Wings"

This allusion to the force of the wind makes me think of what we used to do a long time ago. Our car was old, the gas was almost gone, and we hardly had enough brakes on the car to stop it. We would climb up a hill, put the car in neutral and coast down. Just as we reached the bottom of the hill, we would press lightly on the gas pedal. The motor would pick up and we would travel on. There was a lift to this kind of driving and the coasting was always fun.

Jesus can make our daily lives just this exhilarating. We have all had times when we were struggling with some obstacle and all at once, an unseen force took the work out of it. God has a way of knowing when we need His help and most of the time, He will let us exhaust every ounce of strength we have before He puts His shoulder to the wheel. Other times, He may relieve our burdens before we feel that we have reached the point of complete exhaustion. When this happens, we have had an extra blessing for the day.

Our Church used to have a kite flying day early in the spring. We would gather in a large, open field and prepare our kites for flying. Just as we got up speed and came sprinting down the flyway, the wind would take a corner of our kite and have it straining to get free of the string holding it captive. This was always a magical moment. We, holding the string, knew that we must hold on to the cloth restraints or our kite would blow away. The kite, being an inanimate object, did not understand that the only way it had any purpose was to be held by the string, and carried along by the wind. It had to meet certain criteria to fulfill its purpose – which was to fly. The only way we knew whether or not it would fly was to test it.

The only way we can know whether or not we can fly is to "run with the wind." The 2004 Summer Olympics had many athletes trying to break previous records and set new ones. They only traveled to Greece to be part of the United States Official Team when they had proved their right to participate. We have opportunities every day to "try our wings." The story as told in Jonathan Livingston Seagull by Richard Bach is more than a fairy tale. This seagull was a special bird – he could not live by accepting the standards of the other birds in the group. Jonathan believed that he could learn to soar in the blue sky and not to just hang around with the others and barely get his feet off the ground. He dared to try and found that "the wind was beneath his wings." Not only did he learn to enjoy life as it was meant to be, he inspired some of the other birds and they, too, found the secret of abundant living.

We can just meander along every day or we can dare to believe that God has a special flyway ready for us to use. This kind of flying is not to help us run away from our problems; rather, it is the avenue where we can be refreshed and made ready to deal effectively with whatever is before us. We have never been told by God that life would hold no hard times. But, we have been led to believe, and have experienced it a few times – that there really is a pot of gold at the end of the rainbow. And, if we will only lift our eyes from ourselves, we will find special work for us to do that will bring its own reward. Our own lives may be running quite smoothly right now – but others may be having a particularly hard time. Their trouble is our trouble and what a blessing to be able to help them in even the smallest way.

God created the wind and sends it in any direction He chooses. Proverbs 30 v 4,(NLT) asserts God's ownership of our entire world – "Who but God goes up to heaven and comes back down? Who holds the wind in his fists? Who wraps up the oceans in his cloak? Who has created the whole world? What is his name – and his son's name? Tell me if you know!"

This is the privilege He affords us – to tell the world about God. This is the knowledge that can help us try to fly and by so doing, find that "Jesus really is the wind beneath our wings."

"Does God Really Have a Plan for Our Lives"

God has a reason for each of us being here – "here" being in this world. I do not know what you are to be, or do, because our Heavenly Father is the Creator. Romans 8 v 28, (NLT) is a verse from which we can draw comfort and at the same time, learn to be happy with letting God do the leading.

"And we know that God causes everything to work together
for the good of those who love God
and are called according to his purpose for them."

I read this verse in several different versions of the Bible, and though
the meaning may be the same, this translation seemed to speak of visible
and hidden truths instilled just for you – and me. This was the only
translation I found that specifically ended with saying that we are called
according to God's purpose for us. This is inferred all the way through
– things don't just happen – God permits them to happen for our good
and the good of others. In order to be on the receiving end of this
momentous blessing, we must love God and be called according to his
purpose for us.

This calling is a very personal thing. Your place in the world; your purpose for being here and the work that God has set before you is "your
purpose." My purpose may be different but it is "mine." Each of us
must find our way to make life all it can, and should be. Our birth; the
way we live our lives; and even the set hour of when we are to die, are
all calculated with God's purpose as the leading indicator. If we could
know all the inner-workings of God's plan for our lives, it would probably "blow our minds."

We are not to view God as a hard "task-master." He is as the song says
a "Gentle Savior." His Presence with us is so soft, so soothing and so
gentle that it could bear the description of a hovering hummingbird. We
cannot see God, as we see the humming-bird trying to draw up the nec-
tar in the flower. We cannot hear the rhythm of angel wings fluttering
over our head just as we cannot hear the whir of the bird's tiny wings.
But, just because we cannot see God with our eyes and cannot hear Him
with our ears doesn't mean that He is not here with us. The miracle of
this is that God helps us to know that this closeness we are feeling inside
is really an awareness of His Presence. He wants us to realize that in
every circumstance of life, whatever happens may not be started by
Him, but it is always permitted to touch us according to His plan for us.
Not only does He see yesterday; today and tomorrow are all within His
sight. God never wants us to be hurt and He will always wrap up our
wounds. He knows exactly how far to let us be tested; He know just
how much we can take, without breaking, and we can trust Him with all
that we are, and with all that we hope to be.

I am so glad that His purpose for us is real. This is not some religious mumbo jumbo. We can know that He is a part of everything in our lives and that He sends good our way because He does love us and assumes responsibility for filling our lives with contentment. The peace that God brings to us when He visits can be absorbed into our hearts and minds and can keep us moving on! He does not wish to just visit us sometimes – He wants to move in permanently and have His own room in our hearts.

"God's Mercies are New Every Morning"

When I first got my cell phone, I quickly learned that all companies do not have the same criteria. My plan gave me 500 week-end minutes every month for the quoted price. If I used more minutes than this, I had to pay for the extra minutes used at their rate. But, here is where the catch came in – if I did not use the full 500 minutes, I still had to pay the same price as if I had used them all. Some of my folks could "roll-over" what minutes they did not use in their plan and this helped them the next month. But, there was no "roll-over" with my company –"each month set on its own bottom."

I have been thinking of just how God deals with us in our lives. All month long, He stays with us; comforts us; guides us; keeps us safe from all harm and even gets down on our level and lets us know that He is right beside us. Regardless of how many minutes He uses in our behalf, He keeps no record. We do not have to worry that we will go over our limit. "Roll-over" time is not even in His vocabulary. He gives us what we need, when we need it, and He can do this because He is our Heavenly Father.

There are many things we get concerned about, even worry a little about their outcome. We all know that worry does nothing to help us and even goes against the way God tells us to live. We are to tell God about our problems and trust Him to take care of them. I always have trouble knowing when I am supposed to stop working with them and just put them into God's hands. Some things He can and does take over for us, and other times, He may expect us to do something. It is always hard for me to know which is which.

80

But, one thing I never question – God always has an ample supply of mercies and they never get used up at any particular time. Every morning, His mercies are always new and just what we need. We never question that the sun will come up and then set at the end of the day; we never wonder what pushes the direction of the wind, and we are never anxious that the moon will fail to appear each evening. This is God's business and He takes care of it so well.

When I wake up in the night, I know that God is with me. When I get up in the morning, He is still with me and when I go to bed at the end of the day, He is right here. Sometimes when I have talked to Him a lot during the day, I am "all talked out." It is so relaxing to me to be able to say, "Now I lay me down to sleep; I pray the Lord my soul to keep; if I should die before I wake; I pray the Lord my soul to take." He understands when our words are few because He knows our frame. Most of us know what it is to be so close to someone that saying a bunch of stuff is unnecessary. It is good to just lay our weary head on the pillow and turn everything over to God. Even when we know that we have done most of the talking, God even understands this. He has been able to get a word or two in and this kind of exchange sometimes precedes our being able to just get quiet and listen.

We can run out of steam but God's mercies are new every morning. "The unfailing love of the Lord never ends! By his mercies we have been kept from complete destruction. Great is his faithfulness; his mercies begin afresh each day." Lamentations 3: 22, 23 (NLT)

"It's Almost Time for Bedding-Plants"

The first of May is considered a safe time to plant bedding-plants. The danger of frost is over and the temperature of the ground is getting warmer every day.

This is quite a job and there are many angles to be considered as to what to plant. We want plants that are hardy and not likely to expire with the stress of heat-filled days. Many nurseries will guarantee their plants, at least for one growing season.

To have a pretty yard, our flowers must bloom profusely. Impatiens planted just about anywhere, without regard to background colors, etc., are always beautiful. They come in many colors and look lovely planted around a tree. But, my favorite of all is the red geranium. I forgot what the color is called but it is sort of like the red that is used at Christmas time. These plants really dress up a yard when they are planted in front of shrubbery or along a long walk.

I do not indulge in this kind of yard beautification anymore because my knees won't tolerate the pressure. Maybe you have this same problem but perhaps you have someone who can do the job for you. I can still enjoy the beauty of other yards and appreciate all the work that it takes to make these plants a showy spectacle.

But, there is one kind of planting that I can still do and this is to partici-pate in the planting of my life in God's world. Psalm 1 describes just how God plants us and how He differentiates between a person who fol-lows Him and a person who does not. We do not have to be concerned with our being planted: Our Heavenly Father takes care of this job. We do not need Miracle-Gro, or any kind of fertilizer, and we do not have to worry about adequate water. The nutrients that make us strong and stal-wart are already in God's blue-print for our lives.

It sounds almost too good to be true but everything God has promised in His Word is ours to enjoy. How can we question God's ability to make life meaningful for us and at the same time, plant us where our lives will bear fruit and where our leaves will not wither. Our time in this world is so short – even 70 years flies by and we wonder where it has gone. This is the way God has fashioned the world. He is mainly concerned – not with how long we are here, but how willing we are to be planted where He can make our lives visible and aglow with something that bears His favor. To follow God in this way puts Him in charge of us and allows us to be planted wherever He wishes us to be. We can then learn that it does not matter whether we are a peach tree or some other fruit tree; as long as we are pleasing God, we are living life on the highest plane that is possible for us.

Psalm 1- The Message (MSG)

"How well God must like you—you don't hang out at Sin Saloon,
you don't slink along Dead-End Road,
you don't go to Smart-Mouth College.

Instead you thrill to GOD's Word,
You chew on Scripture day and night.
You're a tree replanted in Eden,
Bearing fresh fruit every month,
Never dropping a leaf,
Always in blossom.

You're not all like the wicked,
Who are mere windblown dust—
Without defense in court,
Unfit company for innocent people.

GOD charts the road you take.
The road they take is Skid Row."

"Become a Believer"

For the past week McDonald's over at Hayti has had a big banner
anchored near the front entrance. It is very visible and is printed with
big, red letters – "become a believer." It is supposed to make us eager
to try their new "chicken selects." It is a peculiar thing how advertising
affects the general public. Radio, television and even newspapers
declare the value of certain products. And, businesses use part of their
profit to pay for these costly words that will incite you and me to try
something they are selling; thereby making more profit for them.

During this Lenten season, it seems to me that these words very appro-
priately speak to what we all need. This is the season where we are
reminded to "give up" the things in our lives that are not helping us be

all that we want to be. It is possible that we can be tied to ways of doing things that perhaps, in themselves, are not bad. But, if they keep us from walking a little taller; caring a little more about people; and making time every day for God to intervene in our lives; then, we need to reevaluate our priorities. Life is not a play-ground; it is a battle-ground! To win life's greatest struggles, we may have to "give up" our plans and permit God to usher in His battle plans for us.

It is good if we can connect in our minds the time we first believed in and trusted God. It may be that no definite time was realized, but, that our awareness of God just gradually grew and grew until we felt safe. Just as each of us is different, God honors our own individual way of becoming vitally connected to Him. Regardless of how we arrive where we can and do trust God to forgive our sin and to cleanse us from all wrong, He makes it happen. After this foundation is laid, we can then ask God to make us a part of His family and we can be sure of His acceptance. This is how I think that we sometimes "become believers."

There is an advanced way that we learn to "become believers." It is amazing to me how many times I can read a certain verse in the Bible and not really believe it enough to act on it. I am talking about a belief that handles what a verse says and puts it into practice in our own lives. This is illustrated in Mark 9:23 & 24 (NLT). Jesus was talking to a man about being able to heal his son. "What do you mean, 'if I can'?" Jesus asked. "Anything is possible if a person believes." The father instantly replied, "I do believe, but help me not to doubt!"

To "become practicing believers" is something that we are never able to do perfectly. I thought of something I heard about Wal-Mart getting so big that they have no where to go. This was just one person's opinion. I am sure that the officers on the board at Wal-Mart have many ideas about how to make their stores better and more prosperous. Their plans might not coincide with the planning moves of another big chain, but they only have to attend to their own goals. This should be our strategy – learning to live up to what we believe is a job that will last a life-time.

The Bible is for each of us – and can explosively illuminate our thinking about the issues of life. These are God's plans and He knows just how to make His truths viable to us. This is real living and learning and every time we try to live out one of God's promises, we become a little more like "real believers."

As we proceed on the road toward Easter, may we desire to really become "believers." And, believing, may we put to the test every promise of God – not to determine if He is right or wrong, but to actually implement into our lives the magic that goes with being a child of God!

"Somebody's Mother"

The woman was old and ragged and gray
And bent with the chill of the winter's day.
The street was wet with a recent snow,
And the woman's feet were aged and slow.

She stood at the crossing and waited long,
Alone, uncared for, amid the throng
Of human beings who passed her by
Nor heeded the glance of her anxious eye.

Down the street, with laughter and shout,
Glad in the freedom of "school let out,"
Came the boys like a flock of sheep,
Hailing the snow piled white and deep.

Past the woman so old and gray
Hastened the children on their way.
Nor offered a helping hand to her,
So meek, so timid, afraid to stir

Lest the carriage wheels or the horses' feet
Should crowd her down in the slippery street.

At last came one of the merry troop,
The gayest laddie of all the group;
He paused beside her and whispered low,
"I'll help you cross, if you wish to go."

Her aged hand on his strong young arm
She placed, and so, without hurt or harm,
    He guided the trembling feet along,
    Proud that his own were firm and strong.

Then back again to his friends he went,
His young heart happy and well content.
"She's somebody's mother, boys, you know,
    For all she's aged and poor and slow;

"And I hope some fellow will lend a hand
To help my mother, you understand,
    "If ever she's poor and old and gray,
    When her own dear boy is far away."

And "somebody's mother" bowed low her head
In her home that night, and the prayer she said
    Was "God be kind to the noble boy,
    Who is somebody's son, and pride and joy!"

- Mary Dow Brine (1816-1913)

Mother's Day is so special! It is always the second Sunday in May when the freshness of the spring season allows the roses to bloom in all their glory. Corsages used to be worn always on this day and we were careful to wear red roses or carnations if our mother was still here and white signified that she was gone.

I think knowing our Mother's love makes it easier for us to believe that God can love us in spite of our imperfections. This was one thing in my life that I never doubted. I knew my Mother loved me. God must have passed this quality on to Mothers and I am thankful to have had the Mother I had. The older I get, the prouder I am of her. She believed that doing right was the only way to live. She never gave up her day-by-day struggle to cope with whatever the day brought. And, she taught me that there would always be a way "when no way was evident."

To me this poem, "Somebody's Mother", is the embodiment of love, coupled with the relationship of mother and child, and nourished by the love of God in the human heart!

"Climb Every Mountain"

It is hard to understand what the disciples thought upon being told that Jesus was not in the tomb. They had misunderstood all along that He must die to be the savior of the world. How cruel that this person they loved and believed to be the Messiah must endure all that the cross represented and much more – for He had taken the sins of the world upon His shoulders. Figuratively, the "mountains" Jesus climbed were the steepest ever undertaken by any person . The paths were hidden by every method of wrong-doing – put there to taunt His calling and to perhaps delude His purposes. But, Jesus climbed steadily upward and even endured separation from His Father!

The story does not end here – somehow what He did there made it possible for you and me to "climb every mountain." The crux of the Easter story is that Jesus was raised from the dead and this same experience is our inherited legacy!

When we come into this world, we soon learn that many things are not to our choosing. To mature and live a meaningful life, we must decide which path we will follow. It is not always easy to know just what God is telling us. Many things are covered in His Word and when we obey, we find peace and joy. But, it is the things inside of us made alive by the leading of the Holy Spirit that break down whether we really follow the Lord closely or whether we follow "afar off." God would have us be aware of every living thing – even in the animal world. They, too, have a reason for being here and this is to please God.

Perhaps, this is the motive we should all put above everything else – that our lives would please God. I am learning that every day brings ways to solidify our closeness to God. He walks with us as He did that eventful day when He appeared to two of His followers on the road to Emmaus. He eats with us; He spends the night with us; and He loves us by making us aware of what life is all about. Our hearts burn within us – as did theirs and we want Him to stay with us and to never leave. This He does!

How accessible are our mountains because God boosts us up when we cannot get a foot-hold. The rope around our waist is attached to His harness and we cannot fall because we are attached to our Guide. The thin air from the mountain tops is filtered before it enters our lungs and the breathless ascent of some of the climbers is not our lot. God takes care of our every need. All we have to do is to "keep on climbing!"

As we climb, search, and follow God, may we remember the words found in Psalm 119:105 (NLT) – "Your word is a lamp for my feet and a light for my path."

"An Open Letter to All Mothers" From –Your Children

To Our Mother,

Have you ever noticed how we are all looking forward to something to make life better? Any of us can give an answer when asked "what do you want to be when you grow up?" Boys are inclined to want to be policemen, firemen, pilots and astronauts. Girls may want to be mothers, teachers, nurses and movie-stars. Even at a young age, we are looking forward to the coming years when we will be grown-up and doing all the things of which we dream.

I am sure that this stretching forward to be more than we are now is part of our human make-up. We would be pretty spineless if we did not lift our eyes from our present line of vision. Maybe this is part of the "get-up-and-go" that God gives each of us. I believe we need this push for our day-to-day lives, but at the same time, I wish we could learn to savor what we have to enjoy today. Childhood doesn't last long enough, and most parents would like to keep their children young just a little longer. And, when we are children, we're just children – we are busy with learning, laughing and having fun. This atmosphere is very conducive to happiness because we feel loved and secure in the care of our parents.

We know you want us to become God's special child – whether we are seven or seventy. Even the "golden years" give us opportunities to keep on "becoming." Retirement brings with it some lovely changes – it gives us time to settle down; to learn to think; to assess who we are, and to reach out for what we dare to believe we can accomplish. The world seems geared for speed and only the young can fully participate. We, who are in the last of the middle years and also in the latter years of our lives, are learning that victory is not always to the swift. Maturity can not be measured by a report card. And, the standard of measurement is very high because it has to come up to the measure on God's clipboard. When we reach for this higher way of living, there is no shame attached even if we fail. We have learned that we must not be afraid to try for fear of what someone might think or say.

So, we thank you today for all you mean to us. Whatever good we have found has been ours to enjoy because you always taught us that "God can make a way when there is no way." Any differences we may have had are gone. They have been swallowed up in all the living and loving of the past. There is nothing between us now but love and the understanding that comes with time. "You really are our hero" and we thank God that you are our Mother! Whether you are here with us or have already "crossed over," we know that you are telling us to keep on believing in the future, whatever our age. And, we are still looking for our ideal of "what to be when we grow up!"

"No good thing will the Lord withhold from those who do what is right. O Lord Almighty, happy are those who trust in you." Psalm 84 vs. 11b, 12 (NLT).

"What Do You Call Your Father?"

I used to call my father "Daddy." It just seemed to fit him. He was middle-aged when I was born and I never knew him as a young Father. I grew up in a time when entertainment was not as available as it is today. Things that we did to celebrate a special holiday always included family members getting together, sharing a meal (usually at noon) which consisted mainly of home-grown vegetables, fruits, chickens from the yard, and perhaps a home-made peach cobbler. It seems that home-makers in that day always knew how to cook. I think girls then were taught these kinds of things more than they are today.

Whatever you call your father, it is so because of the way we view them. He is always our protector. I can remember when I was little; we did not always lock our doors at night. We lived in a different time and fear of the unknown just did not occupy a prominent place in our lives. I was never afraid then because my Daddy was at home and I felt safe. Today's world is vastly different and we have to be careful how we live.

This man who lived in our house was always busy taking care of us. Money had to be earned to buy food and other things that we as a family needed. Wood had to be cut and carried in and water had to be pumped and brought into the house to carry us through the night. Those pumps had to be primed many times. In case you are not familiar with a pump, to be primed is to pour water into the pump where the piston would produce a seal that would act as a force to eject the clear, cold water. Some of the water tasted of iron and was yellow in color. You had to be careful or this water would make your laundry look like old, discolored garments. But, when you drove a pump and found a clear, sparkling stream of water, I believe it would be safe to say that it was always delicious. I have said this before but the best water I ever drank was from a pump that had been driven in Mr. & Mrs. Franks' yard down at Cottonwood. I was tired that day and it was very hot but I know that there was more to this water than my having a great need. It made me think of God's water that springs up eternally and never subsides. It was delicious but more than this, it seemed to sink all the way down to my toes and back up to the top of my head. I may just have to go back down there some day and see if that pump is still there.

My Daddy not only took care of our physical needs but he listened when we wanted to talk. He was very proud of his family and always taught us to be the very best that we could be. I know he was proud of us when we did well in school and he seemed to know just how to make us realize that there was so much more that we had not learned. This still carries over with me today for I know there is no place to quit learning.

It is amazing how my scope of things has changed. When I graduated high school, I thought I knew a whole bunch of things. But, now the older I get; the more I realize how very little I do know. And, this is sort of how I felt about Daddy and Mama – when I was young, I thought they did not know much but the older I got, the more I realized how wise they really were.

To sum up my Father in one word would be impossible but I guess the best I can do is just to say that he was a "gentle-man." Maybe someday he and I can enjoy a good cold drink of water together and we can get reacquainted. One of the young people who won on the American Idol TV Show had a very popular CD out last year named "The Measure of a Man." The Measure of a Man in my opinion is caught up in my Father's image. All the superficial things that make for popularity are not what makes a man but first of all being true to your own convictions, taking seriously your responsibility as the head of a family, and marching to the beat of your own individual drum – these are the things that made my Daddy so real to me!

Dear God, we thank you for our earthly fathers. We are told in Matthew 18:10 that the angels do always behold the face of God. Help us so live that we too will someday see the face of God.

"The Lord Is My Shepherd"

Because of what happened on Christmas many years ago, we have a shepherd. Whether or not some folks remember that this is Christ's birthday; we, who believe in Him know that had He not been born, there would be no Christmas. The guiding star that led the wise men to the baby in the manger and the songs the angels sang are part of this story.

We need to pray continuously that God will help us keep our hearts clean. This is so necessary for us to experience the thoughts and the motivation that He sends to us. Whatever good there is in us, is a gift from God. I cannot imagine life without God's Presence with us every day. I am sure that this is life's most precious gift. God, in His most intimate way, helps us to know that this is a reality. What a blessing to have a part in spreading the good news of Christ's birth.

The Lord says that He is our Shepherd. Not only do we have everything we now need, but we will have everything we need from now on. This takes in today and extends for a lifetime. He lets us 'play hooky' sometimes and even blesses us while we are doing so. He feeds and waters us with life's most choice blessings. When we become weak and sick, He makes us strong again. This is sort of like the manna from Heaven that He fed His people in the wilderness – we cannot collect enough good health and fresh thoughts today that will last us through the whole week. We have to indulge daily and God always provides for us.

When we want to do the right thing and please God, He leads us. He knows that we are not aware of just which way to go and we do not have the intelligence or the inclination to know how to honor His name. This is why we have to be led as the art for today depicts – we are just as void of understanding as a young, meek lamb.

Psalm 23:4, New Life Version says – "Yes, even if I walk through the valley of the shadow of death, I will not be afraid of anything, because You are with me. You have a walking stick with which to guide and one with which to help. These comfort me."

This version, vs. 6 says, "For sure, You will give me goodness and loving-kindness all the days of my life. Then I will live with You in Your house forever."

I believe that God loves not only us, but animals as well. This beautiful lamb seems to reflect some of God's beauty. May our lives do the same!

"These Are the Things That Will Last"

Life has two main categories – things that are fleeting and unfeeling and things that are steady and compelling. From the time we make our entry into this world, we begin to seek the help we need to sustain us. We soon learn what we need to do to get attention.

My Dad was a farmer and he believed in keeping things simple. An honest day's work for an honest wage was his motto. He never taught us, by word or example, to give less than our best. This was not done to win the praise of others; he relished the truth that he must satisfy the demands of himself and this, he did.

Many of the things we enjoy today in our homes were not available then. I remember when we got our first television and how Daddy liked to watch the fights. It was always a miracle to him how this picture got into our living room. And, the truth of the matter is, most of us don't understand the working of television today. All we have to know is how to operate the remote control and we have all these programs at our call.

Radio used to furnish us with the news of what is happening around the world. It has sort of been superseded by television and now even television is being put aside by the magic of the computer. It seems that everyone is trying to learn to do things faster and faster. I sometimes wonder why we have to hurry all the time. But, I've been told that we have to join the rat-race to stay in the game of life.

Daddy believed that as a family, we should have time to read, to think, and to put this knowledge all together in our minds and hearts. We had time to relax, too. One of the things we liked to do was to make and eat home-made ice cream. We didn't do this every day and it was really a treat. Even turning the handle on the ice cream freezer was part of the picture.

My Dad was not a Church-going man. He seemed to think that most church people did not live up to what they should. But, the pastor of our Methodist Church back around 1950 was Rev. Floyd V. Brower. He used to visit Daddy when Mama and I would be at work. Everyone loved Brother Brower so much – not just the Methodist people but the people in our whole town. Most of the county knew and respected him.

After Dr. Paul Currie came to Caruthersville, I expect he heard many stories about Brother Brower. Dr. Currie was just a young man but I'm sure he saw much evidence that Brother Brower had been here. I believe that Dr. Currie has been the same kind of pastor to the Presbyterian people as Brother Brower was to us and our pastor now, Rev. Dwight Chapman, is making his own mark here in our church and in our community.   He is made of the kind of stuff that produces real pastors and great men.

Anyway, my Dad joined our Methodist Church, was baptized by Brother Brower, and was very sincere about his decision. Mama and I were so thankful that our Pastor had loved Daddy enough to visit with him and to explain some of the things that were bothering him. And, when Daddy passed on, how glad we were that he was acquainted with the Lord and that he was in God's care.

There are many things I will always remember about Daddy but one of the most lasting things I will remember is seeing him walk forward, declaring his desire to unite with the Church. God accepts us whether we are young or old if we are sincere and want to belong to Him. And, every time I think of Daddy, I give thanks to God for who he was and that he was my Dad!

―――――――――――

"God Always Confirms What He Says"

Part of the way we learn to read the Bible is by the way we handle what we read. I believe that God expects us to wonder at its meaning; to try and understand why it was written; who said it; when it was written, and what the immediate outcome was. Only time will reveal the final results of His Word.

"When God began creating the heavens and the earth, the earth was at first a shapeless, chaotic mass, with the Spirit of God brooding over the dark vapors." Genesis 1:1 & 2, (TLB) These truths are so complex that it is a wonder we can understand anything about what happened. How can it be that God planned this world with all it contains – just for us? Just reading these verses verifies that God planned every facet of our lives. All we need do is to look around and everything here confirms that we did not come into being by accident.

This Spirit of God came down from His eternal abode and made a world. By doing this, He showed forth, not only His power, but His need for companionship with us. And, Adam and Eve saw God in a way that we will only know when we see His face. "That evening they heard the sound of the Lord God walking in the garden" Genesis 3:8a.

Perhaps this is one of our greatest needs –" to hear the sound of the Lord God walking in our lives." The Lord God made the confirmation that we belong to Him and that He will never absent Himself from us.

Getting acquainted with God begins a journey for us that will never end. We will never have to spend another 24 hours by ourselves. No person, no power, can move us from Him. Nothing can pluck us out of His hand. Whatever our problems, our Heavenly Father has the answers.

Upon being joined with Him, we soon learn that something is different from yesterday's walk. We sense newness about the world around us and most of all; we discover that our "want-to" has changed. This is God confirming that now we belong to Him.

The garbage truck runs and loads some of the extra weight we have been carrying around from all that makes us who we are. God is still in the business of making us over in His image. We learn to confess our sin to Him, to receive His forgiveness, and to permit Him to cleanse us from all unrighteousness. He confirms this is a real process and teaches us to forgive ourselves and to start over again.

It does not take us long to see that God is the "great physician." These physiques of ours have break-downs; our minds need renewing, and we learn that the "heart" within us is out of tune with God. Our Father has many ways of healing us. He directs our seeking for health and no part of our treatment is too small for His attention. We don't need health insurance – the bill has already been paid in full. This is God's way of confirming the validity of His power and desire to heal us.

The years pass and hopefully we come to the place where God does not have to confirm His truth to us. We just know that He is in the situation with us and that He is working out every area of our lives. We begin to learn to look squarely into the end of life here.

Somehow we know that when the time comes for us to make the transition, God will confirm His Presence with us. This will be all we need!

"On Eagle's Wings"

The "golden years" bring many changes to our lives. Our body parts have to be over-hauled sometimes and completely removed other times. Every part of us ages. We need extra protection to help us along every day – when it is cold, ear muffs for the ears; glasses for the eyes to read and sun glasses to keep out the sun; dentures to replace old, worn-out teeth; and even canes to help us stay on our feet.

These things come to all of us and when we are young, the thought of them makes us smile. But, as we travel down the years, we find that we are open to all kinds of circumstances that bring great changes to our lives. It is easy to fill up with fear and we may ask – "what am I going to do?"

God has every day of our lives mapped out and every base is covered. He knows just how to make us understand what is going on and at the same time, His perfect love helps us relax and trust Him even when we do not understand all that is taking place.

The Song, 'On Eagle's Wings' was written for every child of God. The words and music are most beautiful!

"Animals Are Part of God's Handiwork"

Three brown squirrels, fat and frisky, live in my back yard in the big River Oak Tree. This morning I was parking my car and they were putting on a million dollar show! Two of them were sitting on their posteriors holding a nut in their two paws. They were eating very hungrily, chewing fast on their front teeth. Their tails were curled on their back in a perfect spiral. About this time, the third one jumped out of the tree chasing one of his buddies. They walked on my fence, climbed into the yard and drank water that had fallen from the recent rain. They had no idea that I was watching. I sat entranced knowing that God had made these animals and that they have a real place in our world.

I have been seeing a big chicken hawk between Caruthersville and Hayti for the last few weeks. As I drive along, this big bird flapping his wings startles me and then I watch in amazement as he goes upward and then plummets toward the ground. His rudder is in fine shape and he lands on the wires along the highway. It makes me think of God raising us up on "eagle's wings."

I had purple martins again this year but they are gone until next March. Their song is unique and very melodious. I love to see them feed their young and hang on to the side of the gourds, seemingly with no effort at all. They can fly at a great speed toward the hanging, swinging gourd and enter the door before I can see where they are. And, the picture I always think of with regard to purple martins is the babies, nesting in the gourd and poking their heads out for their mother to put a bug into their mouths.

This fall I have seen several species of birds in my yard and they may be just resting on their way home for the winter. Blue Jays are very aggressive as they try to scrounge for food. Robins are busy pecking areas where they think there might be food. Cardinals built a nest in my crepe myrtle bush but I think they have already gone trying to outrun the cold. Even little sparrows are rummaging for winter food and when I feed my cats outside, these birds pick up every little crumb that is left.

Every time I go to McDonald's, I give part of my biscuit to the starlings and sparrows that come up to my car to eat. I enjoy seeing them. God made all these birds responsible for working and earning their keep. And, I think He expects us to work for our keep, also. Whether we are referring to birds, cats, dogs, or my favorite animals - the orangutan and the llama, God made them all and they have their own place in this world. It would be a drab world to me if there were no animals here, especially my cats.

Animals work miracles every day – in their own way. What a lovely thing to hear a parrot speaking words taught him by his owner. I had a parakeet one time that learned several words – such as "merry Christmas; hello, D; and, Good morning, Janie." The first time I heard her speak, it was a momentous occasion.

God has given us so many things to enjoy in our world and as we begin to think of the upcoming Christmas season, let us thank Him for all the things that fill our lives. If Jesus had not come, we would be most miserable and life would hardly be livable!

Psalm 36 (NLT) speaks very clearly of God's love – not only for us but also for animals.

"Your unfailing love, O Lord, is as vast as the heavens; your faithfulness reaches beyond the clouds.
Your righteousness is like the mighty mountains, your justice like the ocean depths.
You care for people and animals alike, O Lord.
How precious is your unfailing love, O God!
All humanity finds shelter in the shadow of your wings.
You feed them from the abundance of your own house,
letting them drink from your rivers of delight.
For you are the fountain of life, the light by which we see."

"Do Cats Really Have Nine Lives?"

I have heard it said over and over that "cats really do have nine lives."
My Mother used to tell me when one of my cats had a narrow call that
this is the way it works. If one was sick and got well quickly, or got in
the street and recovered after being hit by a car, she always thought of
this saying.

She probably was thinking of how God makes animals and people so
full of His healing power. I wonder how many lives you and I have
used up. Most people who have reached grown-up status have had to
deal with being sick. Sometimes, we did not go to the doctor and yet,
we got well. Other times, we were so sick that we had to ask for help.
Doctors are God's lieutenants and so are druggists. Medicine given to
us by them takes care of our problems. Often, we need to keep taking
our medicine to help our bodies function in first class shape.

All of us have had "close calls." If we think back, we can remember
times we avoided an accident because the Lord was watching over us.
There is no telling how many times we have been in harms way and
God pushed us to safety. Some may think of these kinds of things as
coincidences, but we who know the Lord, know that it is more than this.
I have been trying to start my day with an exchange between God and
me. I am aware that He has promised to be with us all the time, wherever and whenever we go. But, there is something special about this way
of starting the day. Perhaps, we may not get any additional treatment
from Our Heavenly Father by doing this, but I am convinced that this
helps us sense His Presence more.

The other day, I fell face down in the street. I was so absorbed in trying
to catch my balance that I had no time to pray. But, God was watching
and He helped me not to be injured badly. This kind of thing could happen to us and the accident might be fatal. We could not have the time or
opportunity to have an inter-change with God and it is so much better if
we work things out with Him while we are able. It is quite fool-hardy to
live our lives with no conscious connection to God. Whatever our status
in this life, if we leave this world unprepared to meet God, we have
wasted our time here and have forfeited our chance to belong to Him.

Regardless of how many times God pulls us through and gives us another chance to live, there will come a time when "the plug will be pulled." We have to exit this world to get into heaven.   We need to keep our relationship with God open and alive every day. When we begin a new day, we do not know what will happen before bed-time arrives. But, God knows and will be with us, whatever comes.

This can be verified by reading Hebrews 13:5 (KJV) – "I will never leave thee, nor forsake thee."

"Don't Fence Me In"

Fences have long been used to designate property lines. There is just something definite about a piece of property when it is surrounded by a fence. There are all kinds of fences – from split rail to vinyl to chain link. These fences can be used as enclosures to keep out unwanted guests.

Roy Rogers used to sing the song written by Cole Porter – "Don't Fence Me In." He spoke of being free to live as he wanted to when he sang

"Oh, give me land, lots of land under starry skies above, don't fence me in." This is another way to look at how fences can be used – we don't want to be hemmed in by anything.

There is even such a thing as an "invisible fence." This is a system where a single strand of insulated wire is buried underground. It is attached to a transmitter which broadcasts a radio signal when our animals get too near their forbidden areas. The animal wears a small radio receiver on his collar which receives the radio signal that the wire transmits. I think of dogs when I think of invisible fences, but they could perhaps be used for horses and other animals. This is a good way to keep the animals home and out of danger from the highway and other animals. This invisible fence can keep the animals in, but it may not keep other animals out. Many of these systems are endorsed by the Humane Society of the US, and other organizations dedicated to the caring for animals.

God uses many "invisible fences" to guide us as we go through life. Sometimes we don't mind bearing the insignia of "Christian" as long as what we are trying to do isn't too hard. It isn't so bad to be labeled as belonging to God when we are using a pen with washable ink where we can wash off His influence. But, when we get serious about trying to live the "extra-ordinary life," we want all God's "invisible fences" to be attached to us with a "Sharpie", that is with ink that cannot be erased.

God allows us to "try our wings" but when we get near a danger area, the invisible bond between us pulls taut and we hear His "stop – be careful." To be safe, we stop in our tracks and we feel the hand of God guiding us back. To disregard the signal of danger is to forfeit God's perfect plan. Granted, we have all been here and have felt dismay upon realizing that we have disappointed our Heavenly Father. But, His love exceeds our standards and even in the "pig-pen", we see His hand reaching for us. We can read of the prodigal son and even understand in our own way just how much God loves us.

These "invisible fences" are not to make us unhappy but to give us license to walk freely; erect; head high; stepping to the music implanted within by God. Real life is full of challenges – one after another – and some very difficult. But, our life is intertwined with the lives of so many other people who need the ministering touch of Jesus. He may use us to alleviate someone's suffering; someone's pain; someone's need to be loved. God never found a person too unlovely to be loved.

Circumstances in our lives can drastically change from one moment to another. Today we may be up busy doing what makes up our lives and tomorrow's news may change everything. Regardless of everything else in our lives, the need to love and be loved is supreme and is the attribute that attaches us to our Heavenly Father. One of God's recipes for living is found in Psalm 91:14-16, (NLT) "The Lord says, "I will rescue those who love me. I will protect those who trust in my name. When they call on me, I will answer; I will be with them in trouble. I will rescue them and honor them. I will satisfy them with a long life and give them my salvation." For God to do all these things, we must first love Him and trust Him. Then, we will be in line to reap His favors!

And, if you are in need of an invisible fence for your animal or for yourself, there is one available. We all have our times of needing to be fenced in!

"Give Me Something to Remember You By"

Our lives would be so empty if we could not remember the past. We do not have to think about things in a sad, tear-jerking way; we can remember so many light, sweet things that filled our days.

Bobby Darin was a popular singer, sort of in the class with Frank Sinatra. Bobby recorded this song – "Something to Remember You By" in 1961. Our country had come through the second World War and the Korean War and was in the process of trying to make some responsible changes to rid our country of the trauma of war.

As always, any change in leadership, whether it is a country, a business, or even in a family, involves putting new ideas in place that supposedly will make everything work better. The results vary and may depend on the motives and the politics of the leaders.

As we get older, it is normal to remember the things that happened "back when." We need to make sure we have a list set up in our minds that bears the caption "something to remember you by." The words of this song are -"Oh, give me something, to remember you by, When you are far away from me. Just a little something, meaning love cannot die, No matter where you chance to be. So I'll pray for you, night and day for you, it will see me through like a charm, till you return. So give me something I can remember you by, when you are far away from me."

When we are young, we learn that it is impossible not to be touched with losing some of our loved ones as the years pass. It is just a fact – life here does end. Hopefully we can live our lives where those who remember us will find something good to remember us by. I believe it is the little things that make life so precious. A five- cent gift wrapped in love is more valuable than one that cost much money but is sent out without the wrappings of love.

I attended services at the Caruthersville Nursing Home today. Every Sunday a group led by Mrs. Linda McLemore from the Oasis Worship Center comes up there and the residents have "church." I have attended several times when I visited my friend, Marie Robertson. The thing that impresses me the most when I go is that Mrs. McLemore makes it a point to put her arms around each person there and she prays especially for that person. It is so evident – they are all so hungry to be loved and any amount of attention given them is so eagerly received. Isn't this what it is all about? Without knowing how to receive and give love, we cannot please God. I John 4:16b (NLT) says "God is love, and all who live in love live in God, and God lives in them." God gives us plenty to remember him by – His Word is still here; His Spirit is still here, and everything that brings hope to our lives comes from Him.

The thing that we need most is love and God delights in a daily shower-ing of His love on us. It may come from a family member, a friend, our pastor, even one of our animal companions; but however God chooses to bless us somehow helps us feel "we are walking on sacred ground."

So, if we can get a new glimpse of what it means for God's love to live in us, it will help us make the rest of our lives here more meaningful. I want to leave something good to remember me by – don't you?

"It's Time for the Harvest"

"There is a right time for everything:
A time to be born, a time to die:
A time to plant;
A time to harvest"
Ecclesiastes 3, 1 & 2, (The Living Bible)

Farmers in our area are busy gathering in their crops. Last week before the big rains came, they were working day and night to get their cotton picked before the rain drops damaged the white, fluffy cotton. We have seen corn picked; wheat cut, and soybeans threshed. Fall is the time of year that these crops and others are gathered from the fields.

One of the most decorative fields we can see is the "pumpkin patch." Their deep orange color indicates that they are ripe and ready to be picked. Not too many pumpkins are grown in this area but some farmers other places grow them as a real money crop.

Pumpkins date back many centuries. The name pumpkin originated from the Greek word, "pepon" which stands for "large melon." Pumpkins have always been used in various ways. Native Americans dried strips of pumpkin and wove them into mats. They also roasted long strips of pumpkin on the open fire and ate them. Pumpkin pie came about when the colonists sliced off the pumpkin top, removed the seeds, and filled the insides with milk, spices and honey. The pumpkin was then baked in hot ashes.

People have been making jack-o-lanterns at Halloween for centuries. Immigrants from Ireland and Scotland brought the jack-o-lantern tradition with them when they came to the United States. They soon found that pumpkins, a fruit native to America, make perfect jack-o-lanterns.

I think what fascinates me the most about the "before and after" of things in our lives, is the "in-between" time. We cannot be set up to die until we are born. We cannot harvest until we plant. I believe that God designates boundaries around us when we are born and that He sets in motion circumstances that can bring about the most challenging metamorphosis in our character. When we remember that we are being changed into the image of God, is this too much of an assumption? This

104

life-long process is one of deep-carving. We are "prepped" all during our years here with the materials that God has sanctioned for each of us. Just as a pumpkin must have the seeds removed to become a jack-o-lantern, so our Heavenly Father sets up a time to remove and to add what we need to be real Christians.

God uses His own pattern for making us into something that can be "harvested." I have never known a christian that did not want to go to heaven. This is the ultimate for us. Regardless of how many years we are here, whether it is seventy plus or a very short time, God is aware of us and where we are in life. Many times, He does give us the desires of our hearts because He wants us to be happy and to know that these gifts are from Him. But, some things happen that we cannot understand and that we would not choose for ourselves. This does not mean that God has forsaken us. He is still planting and harvesting in our minds and hearts and is getting us ready to make the final transition from this world to the next. During our time here God uses us, in whatever way He can, to bring others to know that His love extends to them, also.

Our lives are to be visible in color as the pumpkin; fashioned in features that are open to public view; and humble enough to be quiet while we are "under construction."

As the pumpkin is a bright colored orange, so our lives are to be bright-shining under the watchful eye of God. Our features are to reflect something that brings God to the mind of others and sets up a desire within them to know Him better and better. I have heard it said, "I may not be all I should be, but I'm thankful I'm not what I used to be." Couldn't this be said of each of us?

"Caruthersville's Wrought Iron Fence"

Sometime during the early part of 2004, there was a lot of activity taking place on Route U, all across the front part of the cemetery. We soon learned that our city had purchased a wrought iron fence. It was beautifully carved and jet black in color. As the work progressed, its form began to take shape and revealed that each road into the cemetery was set up with a large double gate adjoining the highway. Upon completion of this project, favorable comments could be heard as to how it beautified this entrance into Caruthersville, especially when the white crepe myrtle was blooming.

I don't know exactly how many gates are left open, but several of them are unlocked and accessible to those who wish to enter. Other gates are closed and besides making this area very decorative; they protect the monuments and other items that family members have placed on the graves of their loved ones.

It is a habit with me to drive through the cemetery quite frequently. It is not a morbid sort of thing – it is just part of the routine that I follow when I am "laid-back and enjoying my day." The river gets my daily attention and I am always entranced to see the towboats pushing their barges, loaded or empty. This is a special love of mine since I worked for Southern Towing Co. almost twenty-four years and earned my living then and also helped to make my retirement feasible.

But, I had a strange thing happen to me recently. On one of my visits into the cemetery, I drove along one of the roads planning to exit onto the highway. As I neared the way out of the cemetery, I saw that the gates were closed. I took inventory and decided to back-up to where I could take another road. I am not a "good backer-upper" and this was quite a conclusion for me to make. But, as I sat in my car, to my surprise, the gates swung wide and I fearfully make my way out of the cemetery, not knowing how long the mechanism would keep the gates open. Now, I get a little burst of joy when I deliberately try to exit the cemetery and force the gates to open. I guess I should have known that they work this way, but I did not. In case you ever get into this predicament, the secret is "stop on the white line" and the gates will automatically open.

As I drove back down Ward Avenue, I thought of how this is similar to the way that God comes into our lives. I always think of fences and gates as things that speak of ownership. We do not have an actual gate that is part of our human form but we do have the privilege and responsibility of opening all that we are to God's habitation. The fence around my yard has a gate by which I enter. The Bible speaks of a gate at Heaven's door and we are told in Psalm 100 to enter into God's gates with thanksgiving.

A gate and a door may be classified as inter-changeable words. The verse I am thinking of is found in Revelation 3:20, (KJV) – "Behold, I stand at the door, and knock: if any man hear my voice, and open the door, I will come in to him, and will sup with him, and he with me." This verse found in the Wycliffe New Testament reads – "Lo! I stand at the door, and knock; if any man heareth my voice, and openeth the gate to me (if any man shall hear my voice, and open the gate), I shall enter to him, and sup with him, and he with me." Both versions tell us that we are responsible for opening the door to God. He is always knocking at the door of our hearts but we must let Him in!

"I've gotta cut back on the caffeine"

Once in awhile something comes along that helps us see just how some of our habits are affecting us, like drinking too much caffeine. Caffeine is so plentiful – not only in coffee and tea, but in chocolate and colas. Just about everyone indulges in some of these drinks very day. It is easy to form the habit of drinking a certain drink at the same time daily. Most people like coffee in the morning, and we want to have something we like with every meal. Our between-meal drinks usually contain caffeine, too. When we are working, the coffee break we get there includes a cold drink or a cup of coffee. Many of our habits may be injurious to our health but here again, only we know how we are trying to make our lives right in every way. We know that God says in I Corinthians 3 v 16, (KJV) –"Know ye not that ye are the temple of God, and that the Spirit of God dwelleth in you?"

Bad habits are hard to break and good habits are hard to form. Good habits take a lot of backbone to make them a part of our lives where they will work. Take going to church – it is a lot habit and I know that we always are richer when we go. But, if we stay out of church awhile, it gets harder and harder to get there. I know this from experience – bad habits hang on to us like a leech. Even now, after being a Christian for so many years, I have to get tough with myself sometimes on Sunday morning. It is just easier to sleep in. But, I want to say that every time we go to church, God is already there. He connects with us in some way. It may be a song, a prayer, a phrase from the Bible readings, or even some thought deep within us, but God comes and fellowships with us in just the way we need Him. Could there be any higher reason to develop this habit of regular church going?

Maybe one of the most harmful habits we have is that of being caught up in keeping the running lanes of our lives open. We seem to have to be busy all the time and this can surely affect us in many ways. It is a very healing experience to be alone, with no television going, and relax in the quietness of the moment. God advocated this when He said in Psalm 46 v 10a, (KJV) "Be still, and know that I am God."

Many things contribute to good health or bad health. Always expressing how we feel about someone or something is really not a good habit. We need to learn to be careful what we say because words can hurt and many times we don't understand just how the situation is anyway. And, even though we might speak the truth, who made us the judge over anyone? This is God's business and He will take care of His people, in His own time and in His own way.

Even our thoughts need to be washed with a bar of soap. God desires to have a closeness with us that is above every relationship we have ever known. He gives us the secret for this in Philippians 4 vs. 8 & 9, (The Living Bible) – "And now, brothers, as I close this letter let me say this one more thing: Fix your thoughts on what is true and good and right. Think about things that are pure and lovely, and dwell on the fine, good things in others. Think about all you can praise God for and be glad about. Keep putting into practice all you learned from me and saw me doing, and the God of peace will be with you."

"Happy Thanksgiving"

"Once upon a time" – how often have we heard these words used to tell a story! Were we to tell our lives' stories, this beginning could be used for each of us. There is good, and "not so good" in every person – a mixture of tender feelings and an inner awareness of some of our imperfections.

If we were to tell some things that have happened to us in the past, I expect we would be amazed to see how much alike we are, yet how uniquely different we are from each other.

Have you ever heard the phrase, "God threw away the mold when He made this person?" I do not believe we were fashioned on an assembly line – the pattern for us originated in the mind of God. Our genes which make us "who we are" did not just happen – they are a part of our heredity and are inherited characteristics from our parents. The deepest part of our nature is the bedrock of all that God has placed within us. These are "His genes" and what gives us a touch of His Character.

Thanksgiving – when we think of how many times God has brought us through something, we can't help but be thankful! He is the giver of every good thing in our lives. We are born with a need to love and be loved. No one has to teach us what love is. We somehow know when something is beautiful; we know when we feel joy; and that inner something we call contentment – all are gifts from God. He has provided everything we need to make our lives over-flowing with abundant living.

This is a very special day – one filled with the aroma of delicious food – turkey and dressing; all the spices in the pumpkin pies; hot bread baking in the oven, and coffee perking in the pot. But, even more important than the food is who sits at the table with us, and the interchange of love and concern that we have – one for another. If this doesn't help us be thankful, we are a long way off from the abundant life that God has promised us. He is always the "unseen guest" at our table and He wants us to give His Presence its proper place.

"Acknowledge that the Lord is God! He made us, and we are his. We are his people, the sheep of his pasture. Enter his gates with thanksgiving; go into his courts with praise. Give thanks to him and bless his name. For the Lord is good. His unfailing love continues forever, and his faithfulness continues to each generation." – Psalm 100:3-5

"Our Hope Comes From God"

When the new year begins we know that we have made it thus far because of the hope that lives within us. Without this magical ingredient in our hearts that causes us to "expect something good", our days would be full of misery. A person without hope has to be most miserable. And, so are we when we do not know that our hope is tied in with God. He is the giver of our hope.

We can look forward to so many wonderful things that we would like to see come to pass. We all at some time in our lives look for and expect to find healing for our bodies. It may be that we are waiting for a special report from the hospital or our doctor. Our minds may be cloudy with fear but we stretch upward to catch the good news that our affliction is treatable and curable. We may have our times of trembling because a loved one is in trouble and we do not know what to do to help. Whatever the circumstances – God is with us!

God is with us in all the moments of life – from the joyous to the sad. I believe that our Heavenly Father really wants us to be happy and just because He is transforming us into a small likeness of Himself, doesn't mean that every day must be dreaded and filled with alarm. God knows our frame – He knows that we do not, and cannot always live up to His expectations. But, this doesn't give us lee-way to do less than our best. And, when we do our best, this something within us that we call "hope" makes us know that we have touched the "heart of the universe" and have found "the key to life." This is not to be associated with pride – our best may not have been first-class. But, in spite of our below par achievements, we have been granted a peek into the vastness of God's mercy and caring for us.

The pathways to heaven are strewn with all kinds of help to keep us going in the right direction. We must never think that God put us here and then forgot about us. I, as well as you, am getting older every day I live and I know that God has always been on the lookout for us. Just because He is unseen doesn't mean that He is not real. Maybe this new year we can consciously decide to "check God out." Knowing that we need Him in our lives and "throwing ourselves upon Him" mean that knowledge plus faith makes us able to hit the bulls-eye and realize that we have landed squarely on target. No degree of safety is as real as that entered into when we decide to put our faith to the test.

I guess that my main want-to this year is to be diligent in my "seeking God." A person jumping from a burning building knows that the net below will break his fall. Our burning building is "life" and the net below "is God." He will always "catch" us whether in life or death!

Jeremiah 29:11-13 (NLT) tells us how God feels about us.-"For I know the plans I have for you," says the Lord. "They are plans for good and not for disaster, to give you a future and a hope. In those days when you pray, I will listen. If you look for me in earnest, you will find me when you seek me".

"—and the desert will bloom with flowers"

The desert is usually a barren place. Lack of moisture makes these areas void of little or no vegetation . The heat is exceedingly high and with the poor soil these lands are just not conducive to the support of any kind of life.

Every year about this time, the stores become filled with amaryllis, poinsettias, and Christmas cactuses. The amaryllis comes from the lily family and is bought with the bloom not quite opened. This is part of the beauty of this plant – watching to see just when it peeps out from its enclosure. The poinsettia is well known to everyone and if one color doesn't please, there are several more from which to choose. But, of the three, my favorite is the Christmas cactus. Of course, this is part of the cactus family but it has a very showy bloom.

All of these plants are part of Christmas to us. The amaryllis can become a thoughtful gift and very fitting for a person in the hospital or nursing home. Poinsettias adorn our churches and homes this time of year and nothing exceeds their beauty.

The little Christmas cactus is very special with its prickly exterior. It bears homage to the cactus family and although its flower might not be as noticeable as the flower of the amaryllis and poinsettia, its beauty is quite unique. It always makes me think that it, like us, is doing the best it can to fulfill its destiny.

It is hard to believe that one day the desert will bloom again. And, just as hard to believe is the fact that one day our circumstances will be different. Perhaps, we have been living in a sparsely inhabited area – hemmed in by things beyond our control. We may think that our flowers will never open; the rains will never come; and the gentle breezes of God will never blow on us again. But, God is the God of the desert, also. Not only does He know about our present plight - He sees the highways winding across the desert and He is willing and able to set our feet on the road we need. There will be nothing to fear here – the lions and all other enemies will not travel with us. This perhaps is the way it will be someday when we leave this world. But, I believe it can be this way for us right now. Granted, our application of trying to live this kind of life may be juvenile but it can still bring us great prosperity and peace and enable us to experience the blessings of God here and now. Our hands will not be tired anymore; our knees will not be weak; fear will go the other way, and our eyes and ears will be normal.

As we begin to think of the Christmas season fast approaching, let us rejoice in the knowledge that this Christ Child born on Christmas Day is really the Savior of the world. All we need to make it thru this world and into the next is Jesus. This is the real meaning of Christmas!

"Even the wilderness will rejoice in those days. The desert will blossom with flowers. Yes, there will be an abundance of flowers and singing and joy. The deserts will become as green as the mountains of Lebanon, as lovely as Mount Carmel's pastures, and the plain of Sharon. There the Lord will display his glory, the splendor of our God." – Isaiah 35:1,2 (NLT)

"Bless This House"

This song was written in 1927 and Perry Como helped make it one of America's favorites. It used to be that this title on tile plaques was bought and hung in our homes. In fact, we have one that my Mother had and it still hangs in our kitchen.

Why is this prayer so popular? I believe that many of us openly and intuitively acknowledge that we need God and His blessing on our lives. We believe this so much that we ask God for His help!

Our homes are only as safe as our faith in God makes them. Security systems are quite numerous today and they are fine but if we really want to be safe, we also ask for God's blessing. What does it mean when we ask God to bless our homes? We want Him to keep us in clear view where He can and will move when we are threatened in any way. His blessing does protect us, not only physically, but also emotionally, mentally, and spiritually. Any kind of contact with God changes us. To know that He is blessing us makes our spirits "leap with joy." It is easy to get emotional when God's hand touches us. I find myself crying; some folks shout, and all of us have our minds opened as we are exposed to God's way of dealing with us.

This exchange between God and His children is available to each of us. There are those who do not know that this is a personal relationship between God and us. God uses many ways of blessing us and He delights in our recognizing His Presence. God wants us to get acquainted with Him while we are in this world. We need His blessing today while we are here; we will need His help when we depart this world, and we will need His acceptance of us to enter heaven!

2 Samuel 7 v 29 (KJV) – "Therefore now let it please thee to bless the house of thy servant that it may continue for ever before thee: for thou, O Lord God, hast spoken it: and with thy blessing let the house of thy servant be blessed for ever."

"God Is Passing By"

Last night I looked up into a tree in my yard. It was raining and the mer-
cury-vapor lamp was on. The leaves hung trembling in the strong, bright
light. Instinctively, I was filled with the thought, "God is passing by."
He is constantly alive in "the wind."

I believe God gives us many opportunities to sense His Presence. He is
not limited to act as we have always known Him to do. His thoughts are
so much higher than ours and His actions more overflowing. He is
always working to enlarge our ability to see Him in all things. There are
those who would say that the leaves moved because the clouds con-
tained wind. But, when we think of the fact that God created the wind,
there is a chance here for us to see that "God is really passing by."
Amos 4:13, (The Living Bible) says "For you are dealing with the one
who formed the mountains and made the winds, and knows your every
thought; he turns the morning to darkness and crushes down the mountains underneath his feet: Jehovah, the Lord, the God of Hosts, is his
name."

Matthew 9:19 & 20, (The LB) tells of a woman who knew Jesus was
going to be passing by. "As Jesus and the disciples were going to the
rabbi's home, a woman who had been sick for twelve years with inter-
nal bleeding came up behind him and touched a tassel of his robe, for
she thought, "If I only touch him, I will be healed." Jesus turned around
and spoke to her, "Daughter," he said, "all is well! Your faith has healed
you." And the woman was well from that moment. She made herself
available to God – she knew the route He would be traveling and she
was not too proud to seek His help. God always honors our search for
Him – maybe not in the way we think would be best – but in the way He
knows is best! God is passing by today – and we always need His pierc-
ing look; His reaching out to us; and His taking charge of whatever kind
of situation in which we find ourselves.

God knows what my heart needs – and yours. He is not always serious –
sometimes He deals in laughter and this is so good. We need balance in
our lives and being able to laugh is a God-given gift. This is a gift that
can reduce blood-pressure; unclamp muscles; and regulate pulse rates.

Laughing at ourselves is great – everyone makes mistakes. The older I get, the more I know that the world does not revolve around me; nor do I want it to. Someday, when I am "out of pocket", the business of the world will go right on. No one is indispensable, not even to God. He is so wonderful letting us have a little part in His great plan for the world. And, when my time is over, someone else will "step up at the bat" and God's purposes will continue to flourish.

God is not only passing by; He tarries and attaches Himself to us. He lets us know that no matter what happens, He will take care of us. This knowledge can free us from worry and fear about the future. As noted, the wind belongs to God and He promises us a way to live that is beyond comparison – Isaiah 55:12 (TLB) says "You will live in joy and peace. The mountains and hills will burst into song, and the trees of the field will clap their hands!" God is always passing by – as the wind testifies of His Presence, so do the trees in the field that tremble and clap their hands at His touch! May we, His people, be able to see Him in the wind and in the unbridled joy that makes trees clap their hands!

Notes used in Inspirational Thoughts

"Nobody knows it But Me"
Written by Patrick O'Leary

"School Days"
Will D. Cobb

"Time"
Dr. Seuss

"We Only Live Once"
Author unknown

"Live Every Day as if it were Your Last'
Jeremy Schwartz

"What Money Buys"
Master Charge

"I'll Always Love You"
Hans Wilhelm

"Me and my Shadow"
Al Jolson

"This is Your Life"
Henry David Thoreau

"The Power of Positive Thinking"
Dr. Norman Vincent Peale

"Lost and Found"
Dr. Arthur Calindro

"Finish Each Day"
Ralph Waldo Emerson

"Jonathan Livingstone Seagull"
Richard Bach

"The Hiding Place"
John Sherrill

"Henry Ford"
Ford Motor Co.

"The Measure of a Man"
American Idol TV Show

"On Eagles' Wings"
Michael Joncas

"Don't Fence Me In"
Cole Porter

"Something To Remember You By
Bobby Darin

"Bless This House"
Helen Taylor/May Morgan

"Who Has Seen the Wind"
Christina Rosetti

"A Psalm of Life"
Henry Wadsworth Longfellow

"God is Good"
Author unknown

"Look for the Silver Lining"
Jerome Kern

"On the Sunny Side of the Street"
Jimmy McHugh

"Somebody's Mother"
Mary D. Brine

"Climb Every Mountain"
The Sound of Music

"Various Scriptures"
The Holy Bible